FINANCIAL LITERACY FOR ALL

FINANCIAL LITERACY FOR ALL

DISRUPTING STRUGGLE, ADVANCING FINANCIAL FREEDOM, AND BUILDING A NEW AMERICAN MIDDLE CLASS

JOHN HOPE BRYANT

FOREWORD BY **DOUG McMILLON, PRESIDENT AND CEO, WALMART INC.**

WILEY

Library of Congress Cataloging-in-Publication Data is Available:

ISBN 9781394209026 (Cloth)
ISBN 9781394209033 (ePub)
ISBN 9781394209040 (ePDF)

Cover Design: Wiley
Cover Image: © HstrongART/iStockphoto/Getty Images

SKY10073287_041824

To the pioneers of the past:

This endeavor would be incomplete without paying homage to the giants upon whose shoulders we stand: Rev. Andrew Young, Bishop T.D. Jakes, Rev. C.T. Vivian, Tommy Dortch, Jr., and Dr. Dorothy Height. These names and other greats echo through the corridors of time, resonating with determination, resilience, and a vision for a brighter future, not only of equal civil rights but also of economic empowerment and the dignity that comes from self-sufficiency.

To my mother:

Everything I am today, I owe to my mother, Ms. Juanita Smith. Everyone who knew her, even briefly, can vouch for why. She was a spirited, determined force, whose wisdom was far more impactful than any formal education I ever received. I have had an abundance of blessings in my life, but the greatest one was being born her son. She brought me into this world and I was there holding her hand when she walked out of it.

Contents

Foreword

It's difficult to concentrate when you're worried about something.

Your focus ends up divided between the task at hand—whatever it is you're trying to accomplish—and the source of your concerns. Pressure like that makes it hard to think clearly and do your best work, and it's easy to make a mistake, to let something slip.

Financial uncertainly weighs heavily on individuals and families. The stress and tension affect everyone in the household, and can lead to intergenerational consequences, from cycles of debt to negative effects on physical and mental health. And when people are worried about being able to make ends meet, it's hard to see past the next paycheck, and it is nearly impossible to dream about getting ahead and living a better life.

When I think about what it means for people to live better lives, I think about how important it is to help people to save time so they can devote bigger pieces of their day to the things that matter most to them. I think about reliable access to affordable, healthy food and quality goods and clothing to help people save money. And I think about helping people to understand how money works so they can make the most of these savings—how to help people improve their financial literacy.

I learned early on, from both my parents and my grandad, the importance of saving and the value—the power—of compounding interest. Those lessons in money management were formative, and they stuck with me. But as John Hope Bryant writes in Chapter 2, Section I, "financial literacy isn't just about money. It's about the freedom to make choices, the confidence to take control of our own lives, and of our communities, and the opportunity to shape our own futures."

That's the American Dream—choice, confidence, control. Freedom. It's about more than just surviving. It's about living life to its full potential, and when people are empowered to strengthen their financial well-being and make choices that lead to a healthier financial future, the dream can become a reality.

Although financial literacy as a concept might sound complicated or confusing, complexity isn't really the biggest hurdle to understanding the ins and outs of money and how it works. Historically, the problem has been access. The tools to improve financial literacy haven't always been available to everyone. Legal obstacles and societal inequities have prevented certain communities and groups from gaining the knowledge and experience necessary to achieve equal financial independence.

However, the concepts in this book aren't theoretical, and John doesn't write about them with clinical detachment. He has experienced first-hand how a lack of financial literacy, rooted in these inequalities, can shape the dynamics in a family and alter the course of people's lives, and he writes about his early childhood and the experiences that shaped him with honesty and clarity.

John doesn't shy away from the importance of personal responsibility, either. He faces the question of accountability head-on, and makes clear, through accounts of his personal experience, the importance of individual curiosity, drive, and determination.

But what might have otherwise been an autobiography, or a sociopolitical policy piece, becomes a passionate call-to-action to educate some of our most vulnerable populations and steer them away from a paycheck-to-paycheck mentality toward a new mindset and a more optimistic, prosperous future. Because John believes in his message. He believes in it because he's lived it. And he wants to see you succeed.

That's why he founded Operation HOPE: to advance economic opportunity by extending a helping hand to the underserved and the disenfranchised, to support, encourage, and educate so that a more abundant life is within reach, for this generation and the next. It reminds me of what Sam Walton said about working together to lower the cost of living for everyone, "to give the world an opportunity to see what it's like to save and have a better life."

As president and CEO of Walmart, I'm excited that we are one of the companies participating in Financial Literacy for All, because we're all better off when people have the opportunity learn and apply the basics of a financial education and realize their full potential.

—Doug McMillon, Walmart president and CEO

Prologue

In the evolving tapestry of America's history, few threads are as significant, and as overlooked, as that of financial literacy. Financial literacy is arguably the least expensive and most effective tool for community economic development in existence today. Other than a job or a basic means of creating income, it is the greatest tool for personal economic uplift available to each and every individual on the planet desiring self-determination. As you will hear me say repeatedly in this book and speeches here and around the world:

Financial literacy is the civil rights issue of this generation.

It is the first thing that US President Abraham Lincoln pivoted to, immediately after the Civil War in 1865, when he signed into law the Freedman's Bank, which was "chartered to teach freed slaves about money." Unfortunately, Lincoln was assassinated a month later, and the dream died away for a time. But Operation HOPE and I are committed to bringing the vision and mission of the Freedman's Bank back to life and at scale.

This is why we encouraged then US Treasury Secretary Jack Lew and the Obama Administration to change the name of the US Treasury Annex Building (the original location of the

Freedman's Bank) to the Freedman's Bank Building—which they did in 2016.

This is why Operation HOPE launched the 1865 Project, focused on extending, continuing, and scaling the original mandate of the Freedman's Bank—this time for all underserved people, including the struggling middle class of America. We need the working class and the laddered-up middle class in America, and around the world, to grow.

Sustainable growth is my calling, and opportunity for all is my mandate. Financial literacy for all is the means to achieve both.

This book is not just an exploration of simple numbers and accounts and jargon; it is a journey into the heart of a nation, its people, and the dreams that bind them—that bind *us*—together. It's an exploration of how we got where we are today, the ripple effects of our past choices as a nation, and a roadmap for new, better choices for a better economically inclusive, and sustainable future.

As you delve into these pages, you'll encounter stories of individuals, families, and communities. Each narrative, while unique in its circumstances, speaks to a universal truth: Financial literacy is more than just understanding money. Financial literacy is the key to unlocking potential, bridging divides, and crafting a brighter, economically inclusive tomorrow.

Money is emotional; it ties to feelings of self-esteem, confidence, and meaning. And it's the financial freedom for all. This I know for sure. As a prominent banking CEO told me just recently, "John, financial freedom just may be the only real freedom we have, because we actually can exercise some real control over it in our lives."

But why now? Why is this topic so pertinent at *this* juncture of our history? Because, my friends, we—as in the United States of America—are at a unique crossroads. We are in an era defined by rapid technological advancements, shifting global dynamics, growing wealth and income disparities, and an increasingly insecure middle class. There are real questions about how to sustain a middle-class standard of living for anyone over the next 10 to 20 years. And with rising political divisions and socioeconomic unrest, the stakes have never been higher for finding answers. The tools we arm ourselves with today will determine the trajectory of generations to come. This topic is so important because financial literacy is the most powerful and positive tool, we have to solving the problems of today and securing our future.

In the spirit of unity and forward momentum, this book is both a reflection and a call to action. It seeks to inspire, educate, and mobilize a movement around the importance of financial literacy as the new civil rights issue for this generation.

Whether you are white, Black, or brown (as in race), or whether you rally behind the red or the blue (as in partisan politics), my guess is you want some more green (as in US currency) for yourself and your community. In a world expert at what it's against, we must now decide on and commit to what we are for. I believe that is opportunity for all. And so, as you turn each page, I invite you to not just read but to engage, question, and then commit to being part of that solution.

The road ahead is paved with challenges, sure, but as history has shown, when we come together with purpose and passion, there's no obstacle too great for us to overcome. Together, let's shape the future—one in which every individual irrespective of their history or background has the tools, knowledge, and confidence to realize the full measure of their potential to both dream and act. To create true agency in their lives.

To a future of possibility,

—John Hope Bryant

Introduction: America's Upgraded Business Plan

Imagine this scenario: You've worked your entire life, providing for yourself and your family, playing by the rules, and saving what you can. Now, you're approaching your retirement years, hoping that the money you've saved is enough to carry you through, and that your years of hustle and hard work have built a secure foundation for your future.

But here's the reality, my friend. The nest egg you've been nurturing isn't enough to cover your expenses, let alone an unforeseen emergency. And worst of all, it's too late to do anything about it. This nightmare scenario is one far too many Americans face, and it's due to a lack of financial literacy. Think about this for a moment. We live in the largest, strongest, most robust economy on the planet, yet most of our children don't even get one class in financial literacy. No one is telling them (and us) how this economy works.

As I wrote in my earlier book, *The Memo*, there is no instruction manual for anyone seeking to move into the promise of their lives. Everyone is essentially winging it in this free enterprise democracy of ours.

Yet financial literacy is the bedrock of individual prosperity and economic growth in the United States of America. Without it, we cannot fully participate in our free enterprise system, and we cannot make informed financial decisions. We are left at the mercy of an economic system we do not fully understand—and worse yet for some of us, one that was not designed to support us.

According to the 2018 Consumer Financial Literacy Survey, four out of five US adults agree that they could benefit from additional professional advice and answers to everyday financial questions. And according to PwC's 2023 Employee Financial Wellness Survey, 60% of full-time workers are stressed out about their finances.

What I have seen firsthand, coming up from nothing in Compton, California, and now as an entrepreneur and successful businessman who eats, breathes, and sleeps financial literacy, is that it's not a lack of desire or ambition that holds so many of us back from long-term financial freedom. It's bad role models and a fundamental lack of the essential building blocks for financial success, including the knowledge and comfort to talk about money, the tools and resources to better our situations, and the right enabling environment to win.

Where I grew up, there was a check cashier next to a payday lender, next to a rent to own store, next to a title lending store, next to a pawnshop. This was normal, but it shouldn't have been. When you come from where I come from, everyone around you has a credit score of 500 to 600 or worse. And so you accept your reality as the norm and what you deserve. But it is not. Through my foundation Operation HOPE and with this book, I am aiming to break the financial shackles that bind so many to a life of financial suffering and a survival mentality.

To me, this empowering work matches and stands on the legacy shoulders of civil rights, in the public streets of the twentieth century. In this twenty-first century economy we live in today, it's silver rights in the business suites that will allow us to all come up together.

Understanding the world of finance is an intimidating and daunting task, especially given its complexity and the speed at which it evolves and at which money flows. This book aims to demystify this world, offering the insights and strategies that Operation HOPE is using to equip communities all over the United States with the knowledge and skills to navigate their financial lives, because this is what it will take to make America the land of opportunity for all.

Our journey will take us through the current state of financial literacy in the United States, highlighting the gap between the haves and the have-nots. It will underline the impact of this gap on various communities, with a special call out to my community of Black America, given its unique role in our nation's history and development. We will explore the implications of this disparity and its origins, delving into the historical events and policy decisions that have perpetuated financial inequality. I'll recount stories from our past of the systemic hurdles that people of color have faced in their pursuit of the American Dream, including the failure of the Freedman's Bank and racial segregation during the Jim Crow era. In addition, I'll dissect how a growing lack of financial literacy has left other groups behind, including my low-income white brothers and sisters.

Take student loan debt, for instance. If you get a student loan for a financially sound purpose like professional advancement, you could make multiples over the cost of that education in enhanced annual compensation over time. This is the calculation on risk and reward that you must make when considering student loan financing (at least until our public policy leaders decide that higher education is a public good that benefits all citizens, and they find another way to facilitate having an educated majority of the population).

My point is: Whatever you do should have inherent value tied to it. Making good decisions about what to finance and when, being an informed and empowered consumer today, has the power to transform the quality of life for you and your family.

But this book is not merely a diagnosis of our society's ailments. It is an empowerment tool for the average person seeking a better quality of life in the twenty-first century, and it is a social movement call to action! The second half of our journey is devoted to solutions that can bring about transformative change. Through powerful and focused financial education initiatives for the public, intentional community engagement, workforce development, and upgrades in environments, we can bridge this gap between the haves and have-nots, between the financially illiterate and the financially free. We can realize the value of our connections to each other and open up the powerful mechanisms of the free enterprise system for all.

Reimagining the Way Forward

America has built its economy through human ingenuity, constant reinvention, leveraging natural resources, and honestly, a bit of luck. Over the two and a half centuries of our existence as a nation, we've built a reputation for ourselves through steel, oil, and gas, and through innovations of industry like the locomotive and the automobile, assembly-line manufacturing, finance, technology, and the internet, and now AI (artificial intelligence). We leverage these innovations as exports around the world, while bringing resources in to help make us the richest and greatest nation on earth. But what exactly has made America great? And what will make America even greater than it's ever been? I believe it is leveraging our greatest untapped resource and our greatest export: our human capital, and their hope and promise for a better future. Let's face it—America is not a country, she is an idea, and we can make and remake her into anything we like. Here I refer to our unique brand of hope, what we've dubbed the American Dream. We just need to upgrade our software for a new century of sustainable growth and opportunity for all.

How do I know this? At every critical juncture of America's history, our people have mobilized in some meaningful way to help cure the "bad thinking" that was taking us on a path to nowhere. We have done this by unifying under the banner of an American democracy that is rooted in hope, exceptionalism, and (mostly) good capitalism.

Given the importance of this national treasure, it seems to me that it's in our interest to protect this gem at all costs. America, without her lofty ideals and the exercised hopes of her people, becomes just another country. Her (our) exceptionalism rests in our ability to distinguish America from the rest of the world as a place of mobility, where people can go from a low estate to a higher one.

Honestly, we need to prove that the American Dream is still viable. We need to back it up. We need to show that the place we call home does give rest to the weary and is a beacon of light to those in a dark place. America needs to be a place of hope and opportunity for this generation and the next.

When tragedy strikes, Americans tend to rally together for the common good and pull each other up. Unfortunately, when the tragedy involves minority groups or someone outside of our interconnected social fabric, the motivation has been shortlived, and the impact is diminished due to our unresolved pain, shared confusion, and in many ways our moral laziness. We just don't want to do the work. We want *someone, somewhere else*, to do it for us. But as you know, life does not work that way. We solve very little by expecting someone else to take care of our problems. Said another way: No one washes rental cars. Most people will drive a rental car until the wheels come off and they can't see through the dirt on the windshield. Then they'll return it to the owner for cleaning and maintenance. The only way we solve our problems is to own them first. The reality is that love, freedom, and equality take work. Nothing good comes easy. Only in the dictionary does the word "success" come before the word "work."

We should be properly motivated to solve our problems today because it's no longer practical or rational to pass our problems on to someone else and because it is becoming increasingly obvious that we need each other for sustained success in whatever this next chapter of American Exceptionalism looks like. Traditional minority groups represent more than 40% of American demographics today, and there are no longer enough college-educated, highly successful white men to drive GDP (Gross Domestic Product, or the nation's national economic output) alone over the next 25 to 30 years. By the way, this is not a racial commentary by me. I have no emotions about the statement, whatsoever, as I want everyone to be able succeed now and into the future. These are just the cold hard facts of the matter. To quote my friend Mellody Hobson of Ariel Investments, "I like math because it doesn't have an opinion." Adding to this problem of passing the buck is the fact that the American middle class is exhausted and looking for an energy recharge (and maybe a pay raise as corporate revenues rise). We can no longer depend on the middle class to sustain the entire economy.

Division no longer works as a business case, and we have far too many individuals struggling to survive, with low levels of applicable education and applicable financial and economic skills for the road ahead, while sitting in what amounts to our shared economic driver's seat, individuals with no owner's manual or driving lessons. The way forward requires equipping these individuals with the knowledge and tools they need to drive our economy. The good news is also that most everyone wants to have a sustainable economy, so we just need to harness that untapped energy reservoir for good.

The way I see it, you can get angry about it (systemic inequality, discrimination, selfish choices, and so on), or you can do something to change it. In every generation you'll find bad actors who are determined to corrupt goodness and disrupt the flow of love. Like it or not, it's up to the rest us to identify it, uproot it, and stamp it out. Next is the most important step. We must replace the bad actors and the system that allows them to thrive with a new one that fits the type of nation we aspired to be in our founding documents, one in which we each have the power and (financial) freedom to pursue our own paths.

That's where we are today. The problem and the bad actors? Identifying them was the easy part. Now we're in the process of uprooting the old system and replacing it with a new one that lives up to the promise of the American Dream. I think of it as our upgraded business plan.

Financial literacy is a cornerstone of this new business plan, and it can be made accessible to all.

As we turn the page on this introduction and dive into the story of when the light bulb of financial freedom turned on for nine-year-old me, let's embrace a sense of urgency, hope, and optimism. Because the fight for financial literacy is the civil rights issue of our time. It is the key to unlocking opportunity, to leveling the playing field, and to ensuring that the American Dream is within reach for all.

Dreams, Decisions, and Destinies

Everything I know, I learned when I was a child.

When I was five years old, I saw my parents, who built a mini empire with nothing more than high school educations, manage to destroy it all in divorce.

By the time I was five, my industrious mom and dad had acquired a family home in South Central Los Angeles, purchased a gas station at the southeast corner of Normandie and Rodeo Road, and ran an eight-unit apartment building on Santa Barbara Boulevard (now Martin Luther King Jr. Boulevard). They bought the apartment building for $18,000 with a monthly payment of less than $250 per month. The monthly rent from two of our rental units was more than enough to cover the mortgage payment. On top of those assets, they had a cement masonry business and a childcare nursery business.

And they lost it all. Everything. The apartment building alone would be worth more than $6 million today.

My dad could make it, but he couldn't keep it. He confused making money with making a profit. He confused cash flow with building something sustainable, with building wealth. He didn't see my mother as a true partner, even though she had the gifts and talents in that area that he did not. He could hustle, and he could make it, but she could save it and grow it.

Here's a little secret that no one successful tells you.

You make money during the day, but you build wealth in your sleep. It's called compounding. You *only* build wealth in your sleep.

My mother knew that.

In a relationship, two plus two should equal more than four. It should equal at least six or eight, and you should feel without question that you are better together. If you don't, then something's wrong—and something was definitely wrong in our household. So, my mom divorced my dad and left, taking me and my older sister with her. The trigger was what happened to my brother's college fund. He was the oldest of the three of us. This short tale of what happened with my mom should be to you now—as it was to me, then—immediately constructive.

You see my dad and my mother came from the South, as in the southern states of America. They arrived in Los Angeles with a few dollars, a lot of dreams, and boundless hustle. They both had the equivalent of a high school education, even though my mother had not formally graduated from high school. . .yet. It's important to know that my mother went back to high school at age 62. She *finished* her high school equivalency and marched with cap and gown with 18-year-olds at their annual graduation. This tells you everything you need to know about Ms. Juanita

Smith, who was called home during the writing of this book, at age 88. Love you, mom.

When my parents met in East St. Louis, my mother had just ended an abusive relationship. My father-to-be, Mr. Johnie Will Smith, fell deeply and quickly in love with my future mother. She agreed to marry him because he agreed to move her and my older brother and sister to Southern California.

My mother had a premonition and a hope that the safety of her children would rest in a solution 2,000 miles away from East St. Louis. This premonition came to her in a dream, then found its way into her reality when my dad-to-be came through town on his way to buying a new car in Detroit.

With my mother, brother, and sister in tow, my father returned to Los Angeles. He was madly in love with mom and vowed to take care of my brother and sister like they were his. And to his credit, he did. We will forever be thankful to him for that. My brother Donnie (Dave Darnell Harris) and my sister Montie (Mara Lamont Wright) both attest to dad's unwavering commitment to them, even though he was not their birth father. He was a father figure to everyone under his roof, through and through. Thank you, dad, who passed on to glory on December 31, 2014.

And Then Came Me

My mom and dad arrived in Los Angeles, California, full of new shared dreams and a desire to have a child of their own to complement their family unit. Soon came me, born February 6, 1966, at Good Samaritan Hospital, in downtown Los Angeles. The hospital has since closed, but the dreams birthed there on that day in 1966 definitely live on.

As I mentioned earlier, based on little more than grit, mom and dad built a mini-empire all on their own. Unfortunately, my dad was better at making money than keeping it, confused cash flow with profit, and didn't leverage the financial planning and savings expertise of my mother.

Civil rights icon, Rev. Andrew J. Young, who is also a mentor and friend of mine, likes to say, "Men and woman fail for three main reasons: arrogance, pride, and greed." My dad was not arrogant or greedy, but he was full of pride, and what I now know is pride can kill. He should have asked my mom more questions about money.

Around the time I came into the world, my mother had saved approximately $4,000 (pretty quickly, I might add) as a special fund for my brother Donnie's college education. She wanted Donnie to be able to attend a college of his choice. She wanted him to have what she did not have: choices and freedom. She wanted him to have the freedom to make any decision about his life that he wanted, to go wherever he wanted to go, to dream big and to be able to go for it.

Even back then my industrious mother knew that freedom wasn't free—that it had to be paid for through self-determination. And she also somehow knew that you could not "self-determine" without having finances and understanding money.

That $4,000 was Donnie's lifeline and his future life insurance policy.

Unfortunately, my dad had "bigger" and I'm sure what he thought were better ideas for what should be done with that

$4,000 mom had saved. So, he used that money for his ideas, and he lost it. All of it.

As a result, my brother could not go to a college of his choice, and his remaining options for a higher education were limited. If he wanted to go to college, he would have to go into the United States military, which offered him and others a four-year college education in exchange for an enlistment in the US Navy.

The simple act of my father taking that $4,000 and doing as he liked when Donnie was 18 resulted in my brother spending not just four years or six years in the Navy, but his entire professional career of more than 20 years. He retired from the Navy with honors as an officer (needless to say, he's super smart, then and now), and went on to work for the US military as a contractor. He married a beautiful woman from Hawaii and now lives in Hawaii with his family. All good and Donnie would not wish it any other way, but from a financial freedom perspective, none of this was his choice. It was all pre-made for him at age 18, based on my dad's decision about that $4,000.

While my brother has had and continues to have a great and very fulfilling life with a loving wife and family by his side, I can't help but wonder what would have happened had he been able to attend a college of his choice and to pursue a passion or profession of his liking. What direction would he have gone in professionally? Would he have been a schoolteacher, an engineer, a general manager of a hotel, or a small business owner? We will never know. That decision was taken away from him.

My mother decided to divorce my father after this $4,000 incident, along with the resulting and interconnected domestic abuse fights between them. I guess she had had enough. She wanted to make sure that her remaining two children at home, myself and my older sister Montie, could make whatever decisions we wanted to make for the rest of our lives. Decisions that she had been unable to make around her own self-determination growing up (as a result of her parents).

A Man Named O.C.

So mom struck out on her own, temporarily moving in with a girlfriend of hers and that girlfriend's man. To make us feel more comfortable, she described them as my aunt and uncle or something. What I remember was a man named O.C., who I now know was my mother's friend's boyfriend. Unfortunately, I never got his full name.

O.C. became everything to me pretty quickly. One day, I fell backward while playing on the front porch and began to swallow my tongue and choke. O.C. cleared my throat and breathing passage, saving me from choking to death. I would have died, right then and there on that front porch, and my story—my full life story as you know it today—would have been over.

That man cleared my blocked throat passage, saved my life, and instantly became my life hero. I would wait eagerly for him to come home from his job every day. But there were some things I did not know, important things about his life that he had chosen to leave out of our shared story. They were about money and how he made his.

Like my dad, O.C.'s pride led to his downfall. He didn't want to share with us that he didn't have enough money to go around—enough to take care of him and his girl, and now these three visitors in their home. He decided to deal with it all inside himself as the self-described head of household.

What O.C. should have done was sit all of us down at the table one evening. He should have discussed how costs were going up in the house and by how much. He should have asked us to come up with a plan—together—about how we could make sure we were not a drain and a pain. He should have asked us to work with him to meet our shared obligations.

If O.C. had asked, we would have worked it out. My mother was working, and she would have been happy to contribute to the family that had taken us in after her breakup with Dad. But this critical conversation, and shared call to action, never happened. Instead, O.C. decided he was going to solve these money problems all by himself by making some additional money on the side. His idea was to sell a little low-end drugs: marijuana.

And that was when everything went wrong. Horribly wrong.

Of course, the first problem was that his new gig was illegal. The second problem was that some other folks in the neighborhood where he decided to set up shop had already claimed that corner. They didn't take kindly at all to his showing up, even part-time. And so, they sent a message.

One day, as I was waiting for O.C. to return home from work at the end of the day, I was met with an image that I have never been able to get out of my mind. It began with O.C. riding his bicycle home as he had done every day I knew him, getting closer to me with every pedal as he rode down our residential street. As he got closer, and as I got more and more excited to see him—this man who literally saved my life—I also began to see a truck coming up fast behind him. The truck picked up its pace as O.C. got closer to home. The final image in my mind—the one I cannot quite get out of my head to this very day—is of the truck roaring its engine dramatically, almost right in front of the house, hitting O.C. and literally dragging him and the bike under the truck and down the street until he was dead.

The man who saved my life? Well, his life was now gone. It had been taken for the equivalent of a few hundred bucks. And I will never get the image of his mangled bicycle and lifeless body out of my head for the rest of my natural life. I can see it now, as I write the words on this page.

They killed my hero over money—not even a lot of it—and a beef about a street corner territory that they somehow claimed as their own, even though it was public property.

Not long after, Mom saved enough money (she was and always has been a good saver) to put a down payment on our first home. It was a modest single-family home located at 15502 South Frailey Avenue in Compton, California. It looks super small when I go back and visit now, but back then, and to a kid, it was a large, luxurious corner lot home that was the absolute pride of our new neighborhood. Back then—and now—it was a massive accomplishment for my mother. She had purchased it all on her own, with her own cash down payment and with her own good credit. At 88, at the time of her passing, she had a credit score above 850 if you can believe that.

There were not a lot of single mothers in our poor working-class neighborhood in Compton, California, and my mother, Juanita Smith, was rocking and rolling. With this and other moves she made throughout her life, my mother proved that getting ahead was not about being Black, nor white, nor brown, nor gender, but about understanding the green. She understood the money! And because of that understanding, she made a way out of nowhere for her family. She opened the door to freedom and self-determination for us all. And I have to add, she did this even when those doors were not opened for her and, at times, were shut in her face. What a woman.

George and Tweet

As we got settled into our new home city of Compton, I made some new friends. My best new friend was a neighbor down the street named George who had excellent grades. He was what you called an A student, while I was a C student at best. I wanted to learn from him. I wanted to become just like him—a good student.

Unfortunately, I am not sure that George saw in himself what I saw in him. While I wanted to hang around and be like George, George wanted to hang around and be like our crazy new next-door neighbor, who went by the name of Tweet. George didn't want to hang with me and be my role model; he wanted to hang around Tweet and be "cool," what some of us in the neighborhood called "ghetto famous" (good for three- or four-square blocks of over-inflated notoriety).

George was way too impressed with Tweet for reasons I will never understand. As a result, George began walking and talking like Tweet. He started hanging with Tweet and behaving like him too. Ultimately, he got shot and killed, standing right next to Tweet. So much for "cool," I thought, even back then. Being cool like that has held very little currency with me ever since. "Cool" isn't worth a thing if it gets you broke or dead.

Instead of being "cool," what I have wanted ever since is closer to what my friend Tim Birt describes as being "intellectually dangerous." Tim told me one day:

> People have to decide whether they want to be [ghetto] famous for a moment, or dangerous for a lifetime. I decided I would rather be dangerous for a lifetime. As in wicked, undeniably smart.

Since then, I have wanted a dangerous, supersmart mind. I aspire to be dangerous from the neck up, not the shoulders down.

I had witnessed the death of our family structure and generational wealth when I was five years old, the death of my first community hero, O.C., when I was seven, and the death of my best friend, George, when I was nine—each of them over money and bad decision-making. And I had had enough.

Luckily, I had an advantage that most of my friends and those I loved in the community did not—I had love and active support from both parents. This cannot be stressed enough. My father might have been financially illiterate, but he was on the level. He worked from "can't see in the morning" to "can't see at night," and he expressed unconditional love for me and my brother and sister. My mother was also enterprising and hardworking—both at her hourly job at McDonald Douglass Aircraft (now Hughes) and at the handicraft business she ran part-time on the job. And while no one expressed much love for her growing up, she told me she loved me every day of my life. That made all the difference.

And that's why I say, to this day, at Operation HOPE, the organization I founded to advance financial freedom:

> There's a difference being broke and being poor. Being broke is a temporary economic condition, but being poor is a disabling frame of mind, and a depressed condition of the spirit, and we must vow to never, ever be poor again.

No matter my financial status, I was never poor. And for that, I thank my parents.

The Start of My Entrepreneurship Journey

By my ninth birthday, I had seen and heard enough for two lifetimes. I wanted desperately to find a better solution for success, or even for managing one's own basic life—for me and those around me in the community. I wondered, *What did hope with a sustainable business plan look like?* As I looked around, nothing became obvious. Then a banker visited my home economics class at Colin P. Kelley Elementary School and changed my entire life.

My wife, Chaitra Bryant, says that all human behavior is learned—both good and bad—and the more I think about this statement the more I agree. This one topic could be a book all by itself. The reality is that I can track all of the backward behavior in my growing up neighborhood back to someone who they learned it from. When you know better, you do better. The problem is, we never *knew* better.

Said another way: *No matter how much I love you, my son or my daughter, if I don't have wisdom then I can only pass down my own ignorance.* Out of love, we pass down bad habits from generation to generation. Out of love.

In 1975, when I was nine years old, a banker from Bank of America came into my elementary school classroom to teach financial literacy, or what I like to call, "the language of money." (Unrelated: Bank of America would go on to become one of the biggest backers and partners of Operation HOPE.) It was a precursor of what was to come in 1977, the first year of the federal Community Reinvestment Act (CRA), which outlined and stipulated investment, lending and service in underserved communities nationwide by FDIC-insured banks.

This volunteer banker, who came in once a week for about six weeks, didn't fit any profile or public image that I had back then for a white man in my neighborhood. The white banker was about 6 foot 2 and wore a fine blue suit with a white linen dress shirt and a red tie. This was a *good* suit, not the drab affairs that the white police detectives wore when they came through the neighborhood where I grew up.

This white banker also had a business card that identified his place of work on the 16th floor of a building. That didn't make any sense to me either, as the only multilevel building in Compton was the Compton courthouse, and that had less than 10 floors. This card said the 16th floor! Where in the heck was a building like that, I asked myself? It might as well have been on another planet from the standpoint and perspective of a little Black kid from an elementary school in Compton, California.

This white dude also showed up at school, consistently, right in the middle of our school day—and he seemed to stay as long as he pleased. My mother—my role model for work experience—worked an hourly job with a lunch break and two scheduled 15-minute breaks before and after. The only way my mother would show up in the middle of the day was if I was in trouble with the school principal. This guy just showed up as if it were his own, rather casually controlled decision. I would later have it explained to me by him that he was on salary and could come and go as he pleased as an "executive" for the company. As a *what!!* I asked myself.

Everything about this banker represented deep power to me. It was something I had never witnessed before in my life, and I yearned to understand it. And so, this new relationship—a first with a white man—had begun. This was the beginning of my out-of-my-comfort-zone training in creating relationship capital, which is now a central part of my everyday life. It should be a part of yours too.

It's worth mentioning that almost every contact that my neighborhood friends ever had with a white man back then was a negative one, usually a police officer assuming the worst of whomever they met from the hood. Getting slammed against a police cruiser by a white police officer was an all-too-common experience as a young person growing up in a place like Compton. Things like this predispose individuals and communities to retreat from any further engagement from people who don't look like they do. Fortunately for me, my childhood experience with white people in my neighborhood was wholly different.

There was my white principal at my elementary school. There were some white teachers, mostly women, who kindly and lovingly even, agreed to purchase whatever it was I was selling that week or month through my series of mail-order catalog businesses (think Stacey Adams Shoes and various multilevel-marketing schemes).

Even the time I got in trouble for shoplifting was a positive experience. It was a couple of white men who caught me stealing candy at what was then Thrifty's Drug Store in Compton. And by the way, this was definitely a learned habit that came from whomever I was hanging around at the time. Kids are not born to steal.

The white men, who had been watching me from a room above the store, had the security guy bring me upstairs and close the door. They proceeded to tell me that I could go to jail and about how bad that experience would be. They scared me completely straight from ever wanting to steal anything, ever again.

They never touched me, but they made sure I got the message that stealing was serious and wrong. And then they let me go home. No harm, no foul. They were protecting their store, no doubt, but they also took the time and energy to protect me from myself.

I never forgot that moment, or them. And so, when I was in my late teens and got hassled by police officers who happened to be white, I was able to separate their bad behavior from their whiteness. They didn't represent all white people to me. I learned that there were good people who were Black and good people who were white and that the opposite was also true. The real color I was interested in, especially after my financial literacy experience, was the color green! The color of US currency. In that home economics classroom, at the age of nine, that white banker taught me the language of money, and I was an eager student.

How to Get Rich. . .Legally

After a few weekly sessions, I gathered up the nerve to ask the banker a question that had been burning a hole in me from the day he walked into my classroom dressed like a business success story from head to toe.

"Sir, what do you do for a living, and how did you get rich. . . legally?" I was dead serious.

Without much hesitation or fanfare, he replied crisply, "Young man, I'm a banker, and I finance entrepreneurs."

"Well sir, I don't know what an entrepreneur is, but if you're financing them, and it's legal, then I'm going to be one."

That was my earnest response. And that's literally who and what I am today: an entrepreneur.

As my confidence grew, so did my role modeling discipline. I wanted to dress just like that banker did, so I went home and asked my mother for a suit. She made it clear that she didn't have the extra money to purchase me a new suit, but I was welcome to wear the one suit I had: a crushed velvet, three-piece job with a ruffled shirt and a big bow tie. This was the suit my mom had made for me to wear to church every Sunday. And so I wore that! To elementary school in Compton! And yes, I got beat up nearly every day after school too, but none of that mattered to me. I knew what I wanted to be and I needed to look the part. I found my dharma, my passion in life, and soon my purpose. I was intensely focused on the road ahead for me, which for the first time, I could now clearly see.

As I have recounted in detail in prior books of mine, at 10, I started a successful candy house business. Through simple competition and hard work, I put the local liquor store out of the candy business in just a few short weeks. The owner of that local liquor store could have partnered with me, but he wouldn't listen to a kid, so I put him out of business instead. I experienced my first real-life financial literacy lesson, with a little free enterprise and responsible capitalism sprinkled in. And I was hooked.

But there was something else, even more powerful hiding in plain sight in that home economics classroom during those financial education lessons with the banker. It was tied to what my life-long calling would become.

My next question for the banker was, "So how many bankers are there like you in the country?

He told me that there were about 10,000 banks in America (at that time), so there must've been more than 1 million bankers. I was absolutely stunned.

"So you mean to tell me that there are a million bankers or something, just like you all across the country, working at banks, whose mission it is to lend guys like me with dreams money? And all we had to do was prove that we could qualify for the loan? That none of us would get shot, jacked or worse, dead? All we had to do was to pay back the money, or admit we couldn't and work out a repayment plan?"

Once again, his simple answer was yes.

Well, I didn't know it then, but not only had I found my calling as an entrepreneur, I had also figured out what I was going to be doing for countless thousands of others, for the rest of my life and at scale: Teach them the language of money, how free enterprise and responsible capitalism worked, and give them a chance at "opportunity for all."

This is exactly what I do every day, through the organization I founded, Operation HOPE, Inc. It is the largest financial literacy coaching organization in America, at the time of this writing, with more than 250 offices in dozens of US states, hundreds of employees, and thousands of volunteers.

You cannot have a rainbow without at least a little rain. The transformative work of Operation HOPE is that for me—the rainbow after the storms in my personal life. It is no different than the heartbroken mother who lost her daughter to a drunk driver and created Mothers Against Drunk Driving or my friend the famous financier, Michael Milken, who got prostate cancer, conquered it, and then became the nation's biggest and most prominent funder of prostate cancer research (amongst other outsized successes in his ongoing life of achievement and giving back).

I went from growing up in a severely underserved community and being economically homeless at 18, to inspiring the president of the United States to make financial literacy the policy of the federal government in 2008. To inspiring then–US Secretary of the Treasury Jack Lew to change the name of the US Treasury Annex Building, across from the White House, to the Freedman's Bank Building in honor of the more than 71,000 former slaves who put their money into a bank chartered to "teach freed slaves about money."

Anyone can do anything in this world if you believe in yourself— and you have others who believe in your potential. You can do this. You can have financial freedom *and* be the person who helps others to achieve the same.

Now it's time to be the change we want to see in our world. What I did, others can do too. And together we can do it bigger and better. The first step is reckoning with how we got here.

What's the Issue and Why Should We Care?

Imagine an oasis in a desert, shimmering in the heat, promising relief and sustenance. You race toward it, only to find it vanishing as you get closer. This is what the financial landscape looks like for a significant number of Americans. A mirage of prosperity conceals the stark reality—lack of savings, lack of investments, and a lack of retirement preparedness. And underneath all of that, a lack of any understanding.

> *"To live in a system of free enterprise and not understand the rules of free enterprise, must be the very definition of slavery."*
>
> —*Civil rights icon Rev. Andrew J. Young*

Credit Is a Tool, Not a Toy

Here's the reality that we all must grapple with: We live in a world that demands financial savvy from us at every turn yet provides scant education or resources to equip us with the skills we need. It's a paradox that our education system has yet to fully confront. As a result, a vast majority of us are thrown into the deep end of financial decision-making with little more than a life jacket of common sense.

With this profound lack of financial education, even the most fundamental financial decisions can feel like navigating a labyrinth. Balancing a checkbook, understanding what an interest rate truly means, or deciphering the legalese in a mortgage agreement—tasks that should be routine seem dauntingly complex.

Let's talk specifically about credit. Credit—how easily it's available and how we're encouraged to use it—has played a crucial role in our financial lives, for better and worse.

There's an irony to credit. It has democratized our access to resources, opening doors to opportunities that might have been out of reach otherwise. Credit means a student can afford a university education, that a budding entrepreneur can start his or her dream business, and that a young family can buy their first home. Credit is undoubtedly a powerful tool for growth.

But our easy access to credit is way too easy to abuse, for example, as a bandage for financial strain or as a way to live beyond our means, or as I like to say, to write checks that we can't cash.

Credit cards are synonymous with convenience. In this post-COVID-19 age of Apple Pay and cashless payments, they're a necessity that's become ingrained in our everyday lives. But remember, credit cards are essentially a loan. And as with any loan, strings are attached—interest rates, minimum payments, and late fees, not to mention the impact on your credit score if you don't keep up with your payments. It's way too easy to forget about all those strings when you're swiping or tapping for purchases.

The stats around credit card debt are sobering. They are why I do the work I do at Operation HOPE. According to the Federal Reserve, total credit card debt in the United States was more than $1.08 trillion in 2023, with the average American household carrying a balance of about $6,088.

Let's put that number in perspective. The average credit card has an interest rate of around 23%. So, if you only make the minimum monthly payment, say, $200 on a $6,000 credit card balance, it would take you almost 4 years to pay off the balance and you'd pay over $3000 (50% of the balance) in interest. And that's if you don't make any more purchases with that card!

We've let credit creep into the fabric of our financial lives, often without a clear understanding of the long-term impact. We've let the convenience of credit overshadow the cost. And that's a part of the equation we can't afford to ignore any longer.

Society has transformed at breakneck speed over the past few decades. Technology has advanced, markets have evolved, and the global economy has become more interconnected than ever before. But amidst these rapid changes, our approach to financial education has been stuck in a time warp. We are sailing through a twenty-first-century financial storm with twentieth-century maps and compasses.

Our lack of financial literacy is not an individual failing; it's a societal crisis. A crisis that has ripple effects on our communities, our economies, and ultimately, our collective future. That's why we need to take collective action. After all, knowledge is not just power—it's freedom. And it's about time we all had access to it.

We need to embed financial education into the fabric of our learning systems—starting in our classrooms and extending all the way to our workplaces. This is not just an ideal—it's a necessity. It's the civil rights issue of our generation. I have dedicated myself to this mission, and I believe that with the right resources, determination, and commitment, we can start a new era of financial literacy and freedom.

The fallout of our widespread financial ignorance is alarming. We are a generation burdened with unprecedented levels of debt, struggling under the weight of financial obligations we are ill-equipped to handle.

But let's make one thing clear: The individual is not the culprit here. For many, credit (and therefore debt) has become a necessity rather than a choice, a means to fill the gap between stagnant wages and rising living costs, and for many, a means to an education and increased economic opportunity. And without the guardrails of financial education in place, this financial tool can feel like a toy—easy to play with and without consequence.

It's also important to know that credit missteps can happen to anyone who is either unaware or even just not paying attention to what's happening around you. It happened to me—not even a decade ago—the so-called financial literacy guru guy!

I had taken out a home equity loan for just about $90,000, and the interest rate was somewhere around 14%. The payments were hefty for me at the time, about $1,000 a month. Years later, I was still paying on this term loan, when a very successful friend of mine suggested that I take out a $1M+ line of credit under much more attractive terms. He understood finance better than I ever could, and I should have just shut up and listened. Instead, I dismissed the idea out of hand and told him, "If I can't afford to make these $1,000 home improvement payments, then I can't imagine how I can keep up a $1M+ line of credit." My friend had to lovingly set me straight.

He explained that because of the way this particular commercial line of credit was structured, and the rate at the time tied to such transactions, the monthly payments for the $1M+ line of credit, would be just about the same as the consumer term loan for my now $75,000 balance! I did the math and was astounded. He was absolutely correct, and I learned little by little to commit to always be a lifetime learner. That's precisely why God gave us two ears and one mouth—so that we could listen twice as much as we talked! And by the way, I took the $1M low-interest commercial line of credit and I paid off that high-interest consumer term loan in a hurry! This is but one example of the power of financial literacy in our daily lives.

Financial missteps—like my own—result in lost opportunities to build wealth, reduce unnecessary financial stress, and improve quality of life. But remember, this is not a blame game. It's about identifying the problems to pave the way for solutions. Together, we can shift to a more financially educated cultural mindset. We can rewrite our financial success story, and it starts with gaining our financial literacy.

The Civil Rights Issue of Our Generation

I believe that financial literacy is *the* civil rights issue of this generation. This is a bold statement to make, but I believe it wholeheartedly. Let me explain why.

Understanding the language of money was as central a piece of the puzzle to President Lincoln and Frederick Douglass's peace plan after the Civil War as it was to Martin Luther King Jr. and Rev. Andrew J. Young's progress plan in the 1960s. I believe that it's also central to our current purpose plan, what I call America's upgraded business plan. Securing financial literacy rights for Americans, especially African Americans, is as important to success and life today as the achievement of the right to vote was in the 1960s in America.

The United States has been heralded as the land of opportunity, a place where any person can "pull themselves up by their bootstraps" and achieve the American Dream. The cornerstone of this dream lies in the US free enterprise system, which is rooted in the principles of economic freedom and opportunity. In theory, this system is open to all, regardless of race, ethnicity, or socioeconomic background. But theory and practice often diverge, and in the case of Black Americans, native American Indians, and other racial and social minorities, the divergence has been a chasm.

Far too many Americans, and not just Black ones, don't have the basic building blocks to be successful in our system. Yes, basic math and accounting are part of it. But financial literacy isn't just about money. It's about the freedom to make choices, the confidence to take control of our own lives and our communities, and the opportunity to shape our own futures.

Who is teaching your community, whatever community you belong to, about financial literacy at scale? African Americans were literally denied the opportunity of this knowledge. Poor whites were sold and continue to be sold lies about the financial realities they face. (*Just keep on trucking and you'll be taken care of! Foreigners and minorities are coming for your jobs! They're the problem!*) Today, immigrant communities and our growing Latin American communities face cultural and language barriers to understanding and participating fully in the system. These knowledge gaps are complicating our progress as a nation. That's broken capitalism.

Seventy percent of the US economy, the largest economy on the planet, is based on consumer spending. That's you and me, paying bills and living our lives. Yet there is no systemic plan to educate us consumers about how to create the wealth that runs the country. Frankly, that seems backward and at odds with the way we do business as a nation.

In today's world, no one is teaching us how to run our financial lives, how to create and balance a budget, or how to run a household, let alone how to build wealth. Seventy percent of the US economy is based on consumer spending, yet 60% of all Americans are living from paycheck to paycheck, according to findings from the 2023 Reality Check: Paycheck-to-Paycheck research series conducted by Lending Club Corporation in partnership with PYMNTS. Of course, we need a new business plan.

The Extent of Financial Illiteracy in the United States

Financial illiteracy runs wide and deep in America, impacting individuals from all walks of life. It is a pervasive issue, stretching across geographic, socioeconomic, and racial lines. From Wall Street to Main Street, from Silicon Valley to the Rust Belt, a lack of financial literacy continues to undermine the prosperity and security of Americans.

Consider this: a recent study from the National Financial Educators Council estimated that a lack of financial knowledge cost Americans a staggering $388 billion in 2023 alone. To put that figure into context, it rivals the annual revenues of tech giants like Amazon and Apple. It's equal to the GDP of countries like Ireland, Denmark, Singapore, and Finland. This sum isn't abstract; it's composed of the individual losses that millions of people across our nation suffer. The cause of these losses range from incremental fees and charges, which accumulate into significant sums over time, to poor investment decisions and missed opportunities for wealth creation.

To appreciate the gravity of these statistics, consider the decisions that all of us make: decisions about managing debt, saving for the future, investing in ourselves and our children, buying homes, and preparing for retirement. Each of these decisions has a financial component and without the necessary knowledge, we can make mistakes that cost us both in the present and future.

This might still seem abstract, so let's break it down to a more personal level. Suppose you're faced with a decision about taking on a $10,000 car loan. The dealer offers you a loan with a high-interest rate because, as they tell you, your credit score is low. Without a clear understanding of interest rates, loan terms, and credit scores, you might accept that high-interest rate loan, not knowing that there are better options available. Over the life of the loan, that high-interest rate will cost you thousands of dollars more than necessary.

Say you decided instead to purchase that $10,000 car using a regular credit card carrying a percentage rate of 14%. And then you decide to only pay the minimum due each month. The result is that you will end up paying more than 100% of the original purchase price cost of the car in 10 years, while never actually paying down the principal of the actual car at all. Think about that.

Far too many of us go into a car dealership and only ask, "What's the payment?" Financial Literacy 101: Never just ask what the payment is (of anything) when there is an interest rate attached. Always find out the terms of the loan.

Here is something else no one tells you: A car dealership consists of *three* actual businesses, with the actual selling of cars being the least profitable of the three. The financing and automotive maintenance departments are *much* more profitable!

We can look at retirement next. Many people don't start saving for retirement early enough, often because they lack an understanding of compound interest or don't realize the significant tax advantages of retirement accounts. By not saving and investing early on in life, they lose out on potential earnings that could have compounded over time, significantly padding their retirement nest egg.

And what about if they work for an employer with a funded match 401K program? Without a financial education, they could be walking right past real money in their pocket. If there is a program that matches employees dollar for dollar, that means the $5,000 that they contributed in a year is really $10,000. That's $5,000 of FREE money that's going to get compounded over their lifetime.

With all of this in mind, consider the cost of being financially illiterate when making these one or two decisions. Now multiply that cost by all the decisions you make in your lifetime that have a financial component.

The Silent Crisis Affecting Our Communities

Financial illiteracy is a silent crisis that disproportionately affects some communities. While it is an issue that cuts across all demographic lines, it is low-income communities of every color that bear the brunt of its consequences. In these communities, the effects of financial illiteracy are not just visible, they are painfully palpable. They manifest themselves in the form of predatory lending, poor credit, limited access to the American Dream, and a distinct lack of hope.

Here is a powerful thought for you: Sustenance poverty is a roof over your head, food on the table, reasonable access to life care and health care, and the like. These are things everyone should have, things that society should find a way to make accessible for everyone. It's basic human dignity, and I would argue, that doing this pays dividends and saves society money in the long term by taking care of it on the front end. But that's another book, for another day. I will tell you this much: All other forms of poverty are based on mindset. Because, as Henry T. Ford said, whether you believe you can, or believe that you can't, you're right. And arguably, it's what you don't know that you don't know but that you THINK you know that's killing you!

The free enterprise system is a bedrock of the American economy, a promise of freedom and opportunity. The idea is simple: provide people with the freedom to create, trade, and prosper, and you'll have a society where innovation thrives, and wealth multiplies. However, this system can seem like an impenetrable fortress for those who lack the basic financial literacy skills to navigate it.

The ability to make wise financial decisions, from buying a home to investing in the stock market, is crucial for participating effectively in our free enterprise system. But if you don't understand the importance of credit scores, the impact of interest rates, or the benefits of investing early and regularly, you are effectively sidelined.

It's not just about having access to the tools necessary for economic growth, like bank accounts and credit, it's about understanding how to use these tools effectively. Like I wrote at the beginning of the chapter, many people have access to credit cards, but without a proper understanding of interest rates, minimum payments, and the impact of maintaining a balance, these cards quickly become a pathway to crippling debt rather than a tool for building credit.

Without a firm grasp of financial fundamentals, people are left playing a game they don't understand the rules of. Like trying to play basketball without knowing how to shoot. Like having a powerful sports car but not knowing how to drive it. You have the potential for speed, performance, and freedom, but without the necessary skills, it's impossible to tap into this potential. And needless to say, it can just be plain dangerous to drive a high-performance sports car with zero performance driver training behind you. You can hurt yourself, and if you're not super careful, those around you as well.

That's because the high cost of financial illiteracy isn't confined to individual wallets or bank accounts. It reverberates throughout our economy, slowing economic growth, exacerbating income inequality, and placing an increasing burden on public resources as people who haven't saved enough for retirement or other life needs turn to government assistance programs for help.

This is why financial literacy isn't a luxury—it's a necessity. It's like food and water for living beings. It's the grease that cascades over the gears of the performance car. Without grease on the gears, the engine quickly seizes up. It may even blow up. In either case, neither the body nor the car can run for very long or very well. The high-performance car that is the American free enterprise system needs the grease of a financially literate population for it to run well and for a long time.

Financial illiteracy not only restricts individual growth, it reinforces systemic financial inequality, creating a cycle that's difficult to break. High-cost financial services such as payday lending and predatory business practices, particularly in sectors like used cars and rent-to-own goods, exploit those who lack financial knowledge and therefore have bad credit. These services compound financial strain, trapping people in cycles of debt, and further dragging down their credit scores, a fundamental measure of financial health. Nearly half of Black Americans have a credit score below 620, which severely limits their ability to access affordable credit and contributes to a systemic wealth gap.

I will dig into it deeper later in the book, but I'll leave this here for you to ponder on right now. What if I told you that almost all our systemic societal problems can be found in 500 credit score communities? The problems were often not created there (I touch on why later too, but that's really a whole other book), but this is where they have taken root and where they proliferate. Black and brown and urban or poor white and rural, these underserved 500 credit score communities—economic deserts really—have the same financial problems and the same predatory businesses taking advantage of their financially uneducated populations. There's a check casher, next to a payday lending store, next to a rent-to-own store, next to a title lending store, next to a pawn shop, and a church down the street trying to make everyone feel just a little better about themselves once a week, so people don't go absolutely nuts on society. The pastors in these churches double as informal, unofficial psychologists for those smart enough to admit they need someone to talk to about their financial problems, and probably their current state of depression.

Compare the picture I've painted with what you know of 700 credit score communities, irrespective of race or geography. Stable. Very little drama. No check cashers. All due to 200 points on a credit score. That is the power and the promise of financial literacy.

In a country where your credit score can determine where you live, where you work, and how much you pay for services, poor credit can be crippling. The existence of entire communities of low-credit-scoring individuals isn't simply a matter of individual responsibility; it's a reflection of systemic issues that perpetuate financial inequality. When the focus is on surviving rather than thriving, planning for the future becomes a luxury. Homeownership, higher education, and retirement security—milestones that are part and parcel of the American Dream—remain just that. Dreams.

I cannot solve all the systemic issues and embedded biases in our country alone, or even through a powerful organization like Operation HOPE. It will take important public policy decisions to do that. But I can tackle financial illiteracy. *We* can tear down the financial education barriers and begin to democratize the American Dream.

There are actions to be taken that we can do ourselves, things that are within our power to do and to change right now. There is hope.

How did We Get Here? AKA Stories of Broken Capitalism

Capitalism: When I do well, society gets *better*.

This, my friend, is the backbone of our American economy.

Broken Capitalism: When I do well, everyone else pays a price for it.

As a nation, we're well acquainted with the biggest profiled version of broken capitalism: chattel slavery. Slavery, as with all forms of broken capital, doesn't add true abundance to the economy. On the contrary, it creates an undue financial and spiritual burden on everyone involved. And in no uncertain terms, the bill will always come due because the moral arc of the universe bends toward justice.

As we examine broken capitalism and its effects, I want you to ask yourself, "How could this narrative have been different? Where could we have done better? What are the tools and knowledge we need to create a society where everyone does well together?"

Broken Capitalism and the Black and Brown People of America

CHAPTER

Broken Capitalism and
the Black and Brown
People of America

This chapter could represent a book all by itself. Financial illiteracy—a hallmark of broken capitalism—and the poor are an all-too-common combination.

Of the more than 200 ethnic groups in the United States, I want to bring attention here, broadly speaking, to Latinos, Native American Indians, and of course African Americans. The Latino culture with challenges and opportunities tied to financial literacy that is easiest to single out is that of our Mexican brothers and sisters.

Most of Mexico's challenges and experiences with versions of broken capitalism come, respectfully, from the unfortunate fiscal management of the new republic, sometime after its freedom from Spain in 1821 (and some would argue, continuing until this present day). The average citizen of Mexico was never empowered with their own sense of financial agency. But it's not too late.

Most people don't know that California was once part of Mexico. That's right. Also, Arizona, Nevada, Texas, Utah, and significant parts of five other US states. It gives new context to those of Mexican descent streaming over the border looking for a better life. Their current challenge is around the legalization of citizenship, education, and ensuring that they are net positive economic contributors to the growing US economy.

By the way, most people also don't know that the second president of Mexico, Vicente Ramon Guerrero, was of African descent (a small point of pride and hope). Guerrero was an independence war general who successfully fought the Spanish on behalf of his Mexico. Then, after becoming president, he outlawed slavery in Mexico. This act both led to the secession of modern-day Texas from Mexico and contributed to his being driven out of office.

And then of course you have the well-documented heartbreak of the Native American people in America. Too many now find themselves struggling on Indian reservations, with insufficient education, a lack of financial resources and economic options, social isolation, and yes, a massive lack of financial literacy.

In spite of the challenges, setbacks and clear examples of gamesmanship played against them in negotiated deal after negotiated deal over the years (which ties back to a lack of financial sophistication and understanding of a market economy), there are clear examples of how—with the right set of circumstances and opportunities—to grow Native Americans' financial agency and freedom. The myriad successful Indian-sponsored casinos (my opinion of gambling as a sustainable economic stabilizer for an entire society or population aside) and resorts, underscores this point.

Next, let's talk about African Americans. This story of broken capitalism I know firsthand.

American slavery was many things that should trouble all of us, but at its core, it was the most egregious example to me of broken capitalism.

Throughout history, Black Americans have faced unique barriers to economic growth, largely due to systemic and institutionalized racism. These barriers didn't simply hinder Black Americans;

they shaped the economic and financial landscape of the entire nation. They put us on a path of broken capitalism.

Jim Crow laws enforced racial segregation in the South, making it extremely difficult for Black individuals to start and run businesses or to gain meaningful employment. The systemic racism embedded in the policies and practices of financial institutions restricted access to loans, effectively excluding Black people from becoming homeowners and building wealth. Additionally, educational opportunities for Black communities were severely limited, preventing many from gaining the knowledge and skills necessary to compete effectively in the marketplace.

In many ways, we merely brushed off the human and spiritual collateral damage slavery had on our national psyche and kept on going. But there have always been some among us intent on bringing America's focus more in line with her heart and soul. From our founding, they began laying a pathway to freedom—true freedom—for Black Americans. What I mean by true freedom in this very American sense is financial freedom: an understanding of money and the ability to put it to work for you in the framework of the US free enterprise system.

On March 3, 1865, as the American Civil War was coming to a close, President Abraham Lincoln signed legislation creating the Freedman's Bank. This bank was chartered with the sole mission of teaching formerly enslaved individuals about money. That's what financial literacy looked like circa 1865. Lincoln knew then, as we know today, that having a firm grasp on money is the fuel needed for economic uplift, and that it can secure the future for families for generations to come.

The idea was simple and well-intentioned: provide a safe place for African Americans to save their money and a means to access credit—a first step toward financial inclusion. However, the reality was different, and the failure of the Freedman's Bank turned out to be one of the most significant disappointments in the early quest for Black economic empowerment.

The bank was strategically located across the street from the White House and the US Treasury Department, close enough for President Lincoln to look out the window and see one of his greatest Civil War freedom achievements. . .had he lived to see it. Unfortunately, hate lingered in the hearts of many who resisted Lincoln's vision for progress and change. A month later, he was assassinated for promising Blacks the right to vote, among other initiatives that sought to elevate the social, economic, and political stature of the formerly enslaved population.

Despite the woeful and unfortunate setback, the dream of the Freedman's Bank lived on, at least for a little while longer. Famed abolitionist, Frederick Douglass, who had escaped slavery himself, tried to run the bank, even lending it $10,000 of his own money (more than $165,000 in today's currency). Unfortunately, his investment and passion alone were not enough to keep the momentum going for the new venture. The framework had been laid, the structure erected, and the demand established. However, it failed because of a gamed system.

Following Lincoln's assassination, bank trustees like Henry Cooke chose the path of greed over the uplift of the nation. The bank was overseen largely by white trustees who lacked any understanding or empathy for the people they were meant to serve. They also invested the bank's deposits recklessly in risky ventures, eventually leading to its collapse. Cooke, a prominent, politically connected white man, even lent the bank's money to himself, something that was in clear and direct conflict with the bank's charter and rules.

When the Freedman's Bank failed in 1874, it shattered the dreams and life savings of more than 60,000 Black depositors. To add insult to injury, the US government didn't reimburse these depositors, as it did during the Savings and Loan crisis of the 1980s and the Great Recession of 2008. The Freedman's Bank collapse was a devastating blow, both financially and psychologically, to a people who were newly emancipated and trying to gain a foothold in a society stacked against them.

As fate would have it, 150 years later, I had the honor of working with then–US Treasury Secretary Jack Lew and Treasury advisors—including Amias Moore Gerety and Wally Adeyemo, who is today the deputy secretary of the US Treasury Department and the highest ranking person of African descent to hold a role at the Treasury ever—to rename the US Treasury Annex Building to the Freedman's Bank Building, at the location of the original Freedman's Bank. And next to the Freedman's Bank Building, my friend, the famed financier Michael Milken, is now building his Milken Center for the Advancement of the American Dream, focused on celebrating the nation's aspirations, and inspiring a new generation of dreamers. I am told that the Center plans on featuring the importance of financial literacy in their halls.

The failure of the Freedman's Bank was a bitter lesson for Black America. It was a stark introduction to the harsh realities of broken capitalism—a system that promised fairness and equality for all but often delivered the opposite for some.

The First Reconstruction and the Black Middle Class Saga

The failure of Freedman's Bank is just one story of how America engaged in the cycle of change and uplift, especially when Black folks were at the center, and how we've fallen short as a nation just before making the yards for a metaphorical first down conversion.

The end of the Civil War and the creation of the Freedman's Bank signaled the start of what history calls the First Reconstruction period. It was all about freedom—not just Black freedom, but the freedom of our nation. The freedom to be, to strive, and to live up to our creed. Freedom for all of our shared consciousness.

Unfortunately, that shared freedom was short-lived.

In the early twentieth century, "Black Wall Street" was a powerful testament to the resilience and economic potency of the Black community. Less than 60 years out of slavery, Blacks in Tulsa, Oklahoma, had constructed a fully functioning economy—a microcosm of what could have been replicated on a national scale. Businesses were flourishing. Property ownership was common. There was wealth creation, economic mobility, and a robust Black middle class.

Then came the Tulsa Race Massacre of 1921. White mobs systematically destroyed this prosperous district as an aggressive act of economic and racial warfare. It was a clear signal: Black economic progress would not be tolerated.

The story of Rosewood, Florida, was sadly all too similar. In 1923, this thriving Black town was leveled to the ground due to a racially motivated attack spurred by a false accusation. Imagine the economic potential that was destroyed that day. The destruction of these prosperous middle-class Black communities created a ripple effect of economic setback that spanned generations.

In large part, the period between 1865 and 1965 was a fast march backward for many marginalized groups in America, particularly African Americans. This is not hyperbole or emotionalism. This is cold, hard facts, the math of the matter. Quoting my friend Mellody Hobson (now chair of Starbucks and co-CEO of Ariel Capital Management in Chicago), "I like math because it doesn't have an opinion."

The math of the matter is that more than 60,000 formerly enslaved people, including Black patriots who fought for their country in the Civil War, lost almost every dime in a bank they "believed" was backed by the federal government, as it was created by the federal government. It was not. And they lost almost everything because of the mismanagement of and by the white overseers of the day, who helped themselves to loans designed for almost anyone but them.

The fact of the matter is that sharecropping, and convict leasing replaced slavery in everything but name in most parts of the slaveholding South. Some would argue that it did even more harm, at least economically and as it relates to the aspirations of a people.

At the same time, Blacks were left out of the western expansion of the United States, commonly known as the Homestead Act of 1862, which provided more than 160 acres to any individual willing to farm the land. Of the 270 million acres, the math is that more than 246 million acres went to white families, 96% of all grant patents. About 1.6 million white families received land grants of 160 acres each, while less than 5,500 African American claimants received land patents.

Back then, just like today, land is the central global asset where wealth comes from. Real estate remains the largest business sector in the world. So think of the impact that giving away 270 million acres, 10% of America's land, almost exclusively to white families had on the economic landscape of America.

The facts and math of the matter are that Blacks were run off of the land experiment, known as "40 Acres and a Mule," following Lincoln's assassination. (Special) Field Order 15, which came later as a bit of a consolation prize to African Americans, promised 400,000 acres set aside just for the formerly enslaved. The land was concentrated along the east coast, covering beachfront property from South Carolina down to Florida, extending 30 miles end to end. Each Black family was to receive 40 acres (notice already, the difference in size of the land grant patents, but hold on for the broken capitalism part that's coming).

While we all love beachfront property, and today it's considered highly valuable, back in the 1800s—the agricultural age—it was virtually worthless. Sand doesn't hold planting seeds very well, amongst a host of other challenges. But Blacks didn't complain. They wanted a shot at the American Dream and would use whatever they were given as a foothold up the ladder. They worked that land so hard that within a month of the initial award, Lincoln's team rewarded their "industriousness'" with a mule (like giving someone a tractor for a farm today).

Now here's the kicker. After Lincoln's assassination, with President Andrew Johnson taking over, (Special) Field Order

15 was canceled completely. All of the 400,000 acre substandard property awards were returned to segregationist families, the planters that owned the land and had declared war on the United States of America!

Think, about that for a minute. All of it, please. Blacks fought for their country in a war against people who thought they didn't deserve equal rights under the law. Their reward? Having to give back the land—the land that they had worked so hard to make usable—to the very segregationists who deemed them "less than" and whom they had won the war against!

Slap in the face is not nearly a strong enough sentiment to describe this flagrant disrespect. And this was in addition to the tragic slight of the Homestead Act.

These actions were more than just disrespectful to America's servicemen and veterans who fought to preserve and uphold the integrity of our Union and its ideals. They were bad business moves for America, ones that restricted the growth of our most valuable asset: our aspirations and the economic growth that stems from it. These acts and so many others stripped Blacks of their pride and the hope that comes with being an American with moral agency and the ability to create change.

The Jim Crow Era

Jim Crow plays a particularly bleak role in America's narrative of redemption and renewal. Jim Crow laws controlled the approximately 100-year period from 1865 to 1965, a century of broken capitalism. This uniquely American caste system was how the power maintained their advantages. They protected their

American Dream by denying Blacks and other ethnic and social minorities access to it. It was the epitome of broken capitalism.

Jim Crow was in effect a gift to the American South. Southerners had been the bad actors in an American confederacy, but the federal government still needed them and didn't want to offend their sensibilities. Instead of helping the Confederate South move past the antebellum period in the name of unity, our government pandered to them by allowing for the psychological and spiritual degradation of the Black community. Under Jim Crow, Blacks were given a form of freedom—freedom in name—but were denied full access, power, and participation in the American social, political, and economic systems. This was how they disrupted the good work and progress Blacks made during the First Reconstruction—it goes without saying that it left a trail of destruction in its path.

Moving into the twentieth century, after World War II, the federal government authorized the G.I. Bill, which gave returning war veterans the opportunity of a lifetime: a college education, new job skills, and a mortgage for a new home. This one act alone effectively created the modern industrial age middle class and triggered 60+ years of economic growth and success.

Unfortunately, only a very small fraction of African Americans benefited from the G.I. Bill. According to an analysis and report done by the History Channel, in 1947, only 2 of the more than 3,200 VA-guaranteed home loans in 13 Mississippi cities went to Black borrowers. And these sad statistics were not confined to the South, noted historian Ira Katznelson. In New York and the northern New Jersey suburbs, fewer than 100 of the 67,000 mortgages insured by the GI bill supported home purchases by non-whites.

And we haven't even addressed the destabilizing power of what today we call redlining. More often than not, people I speak with attribute redlining to private banks, but the reality is that our government put this in place. In the 1930s, the FHA (Federal Housing Administration) literally drew a red line across and over areas that they deemed too risky to guarantee mortgages in. Want to guess where these communities were and who lived in them? You got it. Bingo.

No banker in their right mind—be they racist as hell or a saint-like Sunday school teacher—is going to write a mortgage loan for a property or to a borrower that the federal government has signaled exhibits a "lack of safety and soundness." In some cases, the government outright refused to insure said mortgages. As a result, mortgages were primarily made in areas that were deemed "safe and stabilized." Guess who lived there.

To make matters worse, redlining raised values in these "safe and stabilized" areas as borrowers there were thought to have prime "access to capital." The pile-on effect was lowering property values everywhere else.

The Second Reconstruction

Then came the civil rights movement, which lasted from approximately 1955 to 1968, and was led by Dr. Martin Luther King, Jr., with Rev. Andrew J. Young, Rev. C.T. Vivian, and a host of unsung she-roes such as Dr. Dorothy Height and Mrs. Coretta Scott King by his side. This Second Reconstruction period was marked by a laser focus on access: access to the voting booth, access to public accommodations and facilities, and access to jobs and some careers.

In 1968, Dr. King's focus turned sharply to economic justice. Supported by my personal hero and mentor, Rev. Andrew J. Young, King announced the third element of his civil rights movement, the Poor People's Campaign, which was about bringing together the poor everywhere—white and Black and brown together—into one movement about economics and money. This campaign to address economic inequality was a critical turning point in civil rights history. It signaled a shift in focus, recognizing that the fight for civil rights was inherently tied to economic rights. It gave Blacks an entrance to working-class and middle-class economic aspiration and opportunity, and the ability to "cash the check." By the way, it's worthy of noting that Dr. King's most famous speech, given in Washington, DC, some years earlier, was at a march entitled the March for Jobs and Freedom. And in that speech, he stated, "America has presented its colored people a bad check. A check marked insufficient funds." He also famously said, "It's all right to tell a man to lift himself by his bootstraps, but it is a cruel jest to say to a bootless man that he ought to lift himself by his bootstraps." These two sentences encapsulated his views on the struggle of the economically disadvantaged (i.e., the bootless) in our society.

The campaign sought for equality in the eyes of the law and in the eyes of the economy too. It was no longer a matter of securing seats in the same restaurants or the front of the bus—it was about securing an equal footing on the economic ladder. It was aimed at addressing economic disparities for all marginalized groups, advocating for living wages, accessible quality education, and affordable housing. It was a grand vision to redefine American society, not by ignoring the color of people's skin but by acknowledging it, and making sure it didn't limit one's economic opportunities.

Dr. King's dream was of a nation that would not only provide civil rights but also pave the way for economic rights, ensuring a robust middle-class life was accessible to all, regardless of their race. He deeply understood the limitations of having the right to sit at the counter but not having the means to afford the meal. Unfortunately, Dr. King was assassinated before the campaign could gain full momentum. I like to think that his economic vision persists today and finds resonance with organizations like Operation HOPE.

Now, this was just after the middle of the twentieth century we are talking about here. Less than 75 years ago. That means that less than two generations ago, entire groups of people couldn't vote, couldn't even enter certain establishments legally, and had very few and treacherous ways of climbing the socioeconomic ladder. I make this point to underscore the ridiculousness of those who submit that "Blacks should be fine by now." The math of the matter is that this nation was engaged in the broken capitalism of slavery for 250 years, about two-thirds of the existence of the nation itself. And, up to this day, almost 75 years since the start of the civil rights movement, Blacks and other minority groups are still—still!—fighting for equal access to the American Dream.

The truth is that Black Americans have never been allowed to fully participate in the free enterprise system. Progress has been made, yes, but we're still dealing with the repercussions of centuries of exclusion and disenfranchisement. As we reflect on these historical narratives, remember that we're not revisiting history just for the sake of it. These stories serve as critical reminders of why financial literacy is not a luxury—it's a necessity. And it's our collective responsibility to make it accessible for all.

The Third Reconstruction. . .Begins with You

Of course, I wonder all the time, what would have happened to the dream of freedom, for all, had the dreamer not been slain.

I say all the time today that financial literacy is the civil rights issue of this generation, and part of a new civil rights movement, but what if Dr. King had lived and advanced this critically important unfinished work? Would this have naturally led to financial literacy becoming a part of Dr. King's movement? Of course, we will never know, but Dr. King's chief lieutenant, Dr. Andrew J. Young (today, the global spokesman for Operation HOPE), often says,

> *"To live in a system of free enterprise, and yet not to understand the rules of free enterprise, is the very definition of slavery."*
>
> —*Bill Fair*

I agree with him, and this is also the essence of financial illiteracy today. This is also a problem we can solve.

Each of these moments in history was not only an attack on the Black community but also a systemic dismantling of Black wealth. They've contributed significantly to the racial wealth gap we see today. According to the Brookings Institution the net worth of a typical white family was nearly 10 times greater than that of a Black family in 2020.

This is not a matter of individual effort or personal responsibility. This is a matter of systemic failure. It's a failure of our institutions and our society to ensure that all citizens, regardless of their race, have a fair shot at the American Dream. The economic disparity and wealth gap we see in modern America are the echoes of a system that has repeatedly quashed Black prosperity. These historical events have not only shaped the modern economic landscape, but they also underline the importance of economic empowerment for Black Americans. Financial literacy is one of the most vital tools in the quest to navigate and succeed within a rigged financial system.

Despite the setbacks that we've faced as a nation in our journey toward progress and restoration, most of us remain hopeful. It's embedded in our national DNA. Taking the lessons from the First and Second Reconstructions, Operation HOPE is investing in a Third Reconstruction. The Third Reconstruction is about educating the African American community that has never been fully embraced, the Native American Indians whose land was stolen from them, the poor whites who were left behind when we shifted from a manufacturing economy, and every other group that has been left out of the mainstream success participation game, including the whole half of our population that are women. It is about teaching them how to win in America: How to write checks and not just cash them. How to become builders and wealth creators, at scale.

In today's day and age, we need to remember what really matters. Hatred doesn't matter. The real color to be concerned with is not Black, brown, or white (race). It isn't red or blue (politics) or pink, blue, or rainbow (gender) either. The color that will unite us all is green, as in the color of US currency. The Third Reconstruction will be the one that democratizes financial knowledge, making the American Dream accessible to all, and it begins with each one of us.

How Poor Whites Got Left Behind

The narrative of how we got here isn't one-dimensional. It's complex and nuanced, with threads of economic transformation, shifts in the consumer landscape, evolving work cultures, and big changes in societal norms. In this chapter, we'll discuss our poor and struggling white brothers and sisters. Their history harks back to the origins of America the country itself.

Early on, poor whites and poor Blacks actually got along. They were friends in the early 1600s and were only driven apart because of the short-sighted economic interest of the then-ownership class. This entire period was broken capitalism on steroids.

Fast forward to the twentieth century, when poor whites would find their economic footing. For much of the 1900s, America rode the waves of its industrial prowess. Manufacturing industries sprouted, flourished, and provided the backbone to the country's economic growth. This era was characterized by a prevalence of blue-collar jobs: jobs in factories, in shipyards, on railroads, in the coal mines, and at steel mills. Back then, a job on the factory floor or at the shipyard was a ticket to a middle-class lifestyle. The burgeoning manufacturing sector churned out jobs that offered decent pay and, often, benefits and pensions.

The industrial age stabilized an entire generation—a mere high school education and the desire to work was all they needed to access a respectable, middle-class existence. The formula was simple: Finish school, get a factory job, work hard, and you had a fair shot at the American dream of homeownership, a car, maybe a yearly vacation, and a secure retirement. A comfortable life was within reach. Until it wasn't.

Unfortunately, as the economy moved past the Industrial Revolution and into the technology and information age, the economy, and the country (and our leaders) did not ensure that the population of working-class whites evolved with it. And just like in the 1600s, this important group was left behind.

The rise of automation, globalization, and the technology sector in the late twentieth century caused the manufacturing sector to shrink and decent-paying blue-collar jobs to vanish. At the same time, our society experienced several significant shifts. A new culture of social competition, or what I like to call "Keeping Up with the Joneses" was the result of access to spending power without fully understanding how to manage it. The dynamics of earning and spending were changing rapidly, and our understanding of these concepts struggled to keep pace. As a nation, we lost something vital: our financial literacy. This lack of financial education, coupled with an increasing ease of making financial decisions, set the stage for an entire generation without the tools and the know-how to access the American Dream.

Today, poor whites are the largest population of the poor in America. And yes, financial literacy would have represented possibly the most significant economic development tool available to them, helping to boost them into the middle class in good times and protect them from the trapdoor of poverty in bad.

Blue-Collar Work and the Middle-Class Dream

There was a time in American history when "bluecollar" didn't signify struggle or imply low economic status. Instead, blue-collar work represented opportunity and stability. These jobs, primarily in manufacturing and other industrial sectors, were the lifeblood of the (white) American middle class for much of the twentieth century.

Blue-collar jobs were born out of the Industrial Revolution and the subsequent boom in the manufacturing sector. The factories that sprung up across the nation needed labor, and people flocked to them in search of steady employment. These jobs often didn't require advanced education or formal training, making them accessible to a broad swath of the population.

Working in the manufacturing, mining, or construction industries could be physically demanding, but it also provided a fair wage, health benefits, and often a pension. A blue-collar job was a gateway to the middle class, a means of earning a comfortable living, and achieving the American Dream.

Picture a young white man, freshly graduated from high school, securing a job at the local factory. His wages are enough to support a family. He buys a house in the suburbs, a car for commuting, and saves enough for yearly family vacations. His children attend good schools, and he retires with a decent pension. This was the middle-class dream, and it was within reach of many blue-collar workers.

But as the decades rolled on, this vision of the middle class began to fray. Globalization, technological advancements, and shifts in economic policies led to a decline in manufacturing jobs. Factories that once hummed with activity were shut down or moved overseas, and the blue-collar jobs that remained were often lower paying with fewer benefits. The promise of a middle-class life through blue-collar work is no longer a given. Today, it has become a symbol of ambitions unrealized.

The disappearance of these opportunities left a gaping hole in the fabric of American society. As blue-collar jobs dwindled, so did the pathways to the middle class for those without advanced education or specialized skills. This change marked the beginning of a deepening economic divide that led to a deepening social divide. When you take away someone's opportunity without something substantive to replace it, you take away their hope. And what is left in its place? Resentment and discontent.

Most groups felt the pain of this transition away from a manufacturing-based economy but none more so than lower-income whites. They were the ones whose path to the middle-class American Dream, through blue-collar work, was destroyed. With the loss of job security, stagnating wages, and without the education—financial or otherwise—to pursue other earning streams, their ability to support their families was undermined. For them, the economic ladder was broken.

If you investigate many communities throughout middle America, especially industrial communities, you begin to see a narrative very similar to the one I saw growing up in Compton: a sustained lack of financial literacy coupled with a lack of opportunity that invariably leads to a lack of hope and an increase in poverty. This often results in increased crime, increased drug use, and increased domestic abuse, which contribute to an overall decline in family and community life.

Conversely, introducing financial literacy and opportunity to these communities offers a new sense of hope and belonging. These communities who have been affected by the shifts in the economy have a way out of poverty—both materially and spiritually. It begins with fixing the broken aspects of capitalism, a major aspect of which is investing in financial literacy.

Losing Focus on the Goal: Financial Freedom

We cannot overlook the staggering transformation in the average American citizen's relationship with money alongside the transformation of America's economic landscape. But let's get something straight first. The problem has never been spending. In fact, that's what helps drive our nation forward. The problem has always lain in settling for the illusion of success.

What I'm saying is this: We are free to enjoy our money how we want. The vacations, the cars, and meaningful gifts for loved ones—it's all a part of the beauty of America. But our material possessions in and of themselves are not the American Dream. We need to remember that the American Dream requires informed, educated spending—spending with the end goal of financial freedom.

The economy we know and enjoy today is a product of the post–World War II era, often referred to as the "Golden Age of Capitalism." This period has been marked by unparalleled economic growth, higher wages, and increased consumer spending. Look, we all enjoy (and should enjoy) the fruits of our labor, but as a nation, we dropped the ball in providing the proper safeguards and education on how to responsibly herald in this new era of abundance and access to capital. It's a vicious cycle that we see again and again throughout our nation's history (remember the Freedman's Bank?).

Up until the mid-twentieth century, the family model in America had men as the primary breadwinners and women relegated to domestic duties. But as the economy shifted, this model became increasingly untenable. With the cost of living rising and the aspirations of the American Dream expanding, maintaining a middle-class lifestyle began to require two incomes instead of one.

Women didn't just enter the workforce; they forged a path, broke barriers, and demanded their rightful place. They took on roles traditionally dominated by men and became a vital part of the economic fabric of the nation.

But it wasn't an easy transition into this "man's world."

Decades later, we still have a gender wage gap here in America, with women earning less and having less access to higher paying jobs than men. And even as they work the same hours as men, women are still expected to shoulder the bulk of household chores and childcare, what's often referred to as the "double burden."

As women grappled with these challenges, it became clear that financial literacy was not just important; it was essential for their true freedom in this new economic reality.

The introduction of a formal credit system through credit cards began to change the way many Americans operated. Credit cards presented a way to increase buying power; they gave consumers opportunity to make a broader set of financial decisions. This was exciting, life-changing stuff—mostly good, but because of a widespread lack of financial literacy, there's also been a downside.

Think of it like this. If you give a teenager with no license and no training a brand-new car, what is a likely result? Now, think about how different the outcome would be if that same teen were given proper training, practice, and was made to pass a test to certify their driving and road knowledge. That car, which is also in many senses a luxury, is now a tool and investment. Credit is the same. Many Americans began using the tool of credit without fully understanding how to wield its power.

Much like credit, having increased buying power is a double-edged sword. On the one hand, it drives economic growth, innovation, and offers consumers a dazzling array of choices to suit their unique needs. On the other hand, without proper guidance, it can erode financial health and stability.

So, the situation we faced in the late twentieth century was an increase in the desire to buy things, and a decrease in the ability to earn, accompanied by an increase in access to powerful financial tools and a decrease in financial literacy. Sadly, as economic pressures bore down, many were unprepared to face the reality of their economic choices. Without the necessary financial literacy to navigate this complex landscape, too many of us end up burdened by debt, living paycheck to paycheck, with little to no savings for emergencies, let alone retirement.

As we were buying into the dream, we were selling out our futures.

The American Dream Deferred

The American Dream has always been rooted in the belief that with hard work and determination, anyone can succeed in this country. It's the narrative that has inspired generations of Americans to strive for a better life.

But the systemic barriers that have kept financial education out of the heads of so many—in fact, most—groups have made this dream elusive.

In the United States, most Americans build wealth through a combination of homeownership, investments, education, and business creation. These traditional avenues to wealth creation require a nuanced understanding of financial matters. It requires navigating through complex financial systems and making informed decisions.

A lack of financial knowledge not only impedes individuals from building wealth, it prevents them from protecting what they've earned. This inability to manage and grow wealth affects the ability to invest in education, buy a home, start a business, or even retire comfortably—all critical components of the American Dream.

Homeownership has long been touted as a hallmark of the American Dream, a tangible symbol of financial stability. That's because it is. By the way, don't listen to the people telling you on television that you don't need to own a home. Own a home. That said, I can see why navigating the current real estate market and understanding mortgage rates, or even just the long-term implications of an adjustable-rate mortgage versus a fixed-rate mortgage, feels like a bar too high and intimidating for many folks. And these aren't just good-to-know details; this is crucial information to ensuring your home-buying dream doesn't turn into a financial nightmare.

Similarly, investments—whether in the stock market, bonds, mutual funds, or retirement accounts—are key to building wealth and ensuring financial security in the future. But understanding these investments, recognizing the difference between a high-risk and a low-risk investment, and knowing how to diversify your investment portfolio is the language of financial literacy. And if you can't speak this language, you're playing a high-stakes game with blindfolds on.

Education and business creation, too, are littered with financial decisions and obligations. Whether it's choosing a college, deciding on a student loan, selecting a business structure, or understanding tax obligations, every step on these paths requires important financial decisions. Making the right choices along the way can spell the difference between success and failure, prosperity and poverty.

The harsh reality is that without financial literacy, fully participating in the free enterprise system becomes a Herculean task. The rules of the game seem convoluted and the playing field, uneven. This lack of participation not only stymies individual potential but also impedes our collective economic growth.

In the face of rising costs of living, stagnant wages, and an increasing wealth gap, financial literacy is no longer just about money management; it's about economic survival. It's about the ability to make informed decisions that can change the trajectory of people's lives and the lives of their loved ones. It's about understanding the rules of the economic game and using them to your advantage. Next, we'll explore some of the most important ones and how a lack of financial literacy has led to so many falling behind on their dreams.

The Student Debt Crisis

According to the College Board, the average cost of tuition and fees at a public four-year college institution for in-state students rose by more than 210% in the last 30 years, adjusting for inflation. That means that it's more important, now more than ever, for students to prioritize their education in K–12 and make meaningful decisions for how to use their degree in college. Most meaningful investments are expensive. But the goal is to get out more than you put in.

The dream of attending college and securing a promising future has long been a cornerstone of the American Dream. However, the dream shouldn't end at simply going to college. The power of a college education and experience lies in what skills and knowledge you learn in the course of the pursuit of the degree.

In pop culture, college is often depicted as a time for unregulated fun and a time of discovery. It's definitely a time of growth and transition, but it must also be embraced for what it truly is in an economic sense: a major financial investment. Far too many young people followed the advice of their parents, school counselors, and peers, did the hard work of applying for schools, getting accepted, and making the transition to college life, without having real conversations about the role of college in their lives. A college degree should help springboard you toward a better future.

With that in mind, we must teach our students to choose majors not just based on passion (although that is important to a degree), but also based on the job they want to pursue. Parents and counselors alike must begin educating their children on the potential ROI (return on investment) on the degree from the institution of their choice. This too is financial education.

The rise in challenges around student loans also points to another reality. Vocational schools are still an option and are needed in our country. Just like "blue collar" isn't a dirty word, neither is "vocational." In fact, there's a strong case for students enrolling into more trade and vocational schools as lower student debt liability paves a smoother path to earning.

The Paycheck-to-Paycheck Conundrum

We often think the paycheck-to-paycheck lifestyle applies only to those earning a lower income, but the reality is shockingly different. Remember, 60% of Americans are living paycheck to paycheck. If you think that that 60% is mostly people at the lower end of the income spectrum, you'd be mistaken. The truth is that this lifestyle doesn't discriminate. It affects half of those earning more than $100K and an alarming one-third of those bringing in more than $250K per year.

How is this possible? How can someone earning six figures or more be living paycheck to paycheck? Well, the issue lies not in the amount of money they are making, but in how they are managing that money. Earning more money often leads to what is called "lifestyle inflation," where expenses increase alongside income. The higher the income, the bigger the house, the more expensive the car, and before you know it, all that income is allocated to expenses, leaving no financial cushion. Without the necessary financial literacy to manage your income, however high or low it may be, you can easily slip into a lifestyle that leaves little room for savings or investments.

Living paycheck to paycheck is a precarious tightrope walk over a chasm of potential financial disaster. Without savings, every unexpected expense becomes a crisis. A sudden job loss, an unforeseen medical issue, or even a global pandemic can push someone off the financial tightrope, with nothing to break the fall (more on COVID-19 in the next section).

And yet, the cycle continues.

No Contingency Plan

COVID-19 showed us, in no uncertain terms, that a lack of financial literacy is a societal problem, and one that has severe consequences for our collective well-being.

The pandemic has and continues to disrupt lives and livelihoods around the globe, pushing many into precarious financial situations. But even before the pandemic, a significant portion of Americans were living paycheck to paycheck, with little to no savings. The economic shutdowns and widespread job losses that came with COVID-19 exposed the fragility of so many people's personal finances. For those who were already struggling, the pandemic only deepened their financial woes. Suddenly, individuals and families who had been just getting by were thrust into financial emergencies. Millions of Americans, especially those in the low-income bracket, found themselves without a safety net, unable to cover their basic living expenses.

The COVID-19 pandemic laid bare *and* accelerated the undercurrents of financial uncertainty and stress that so many people in the United States were already experiencing. Many families and individuals who were already financially precarious before the pandemic fell off the financial precipice due to job losses and increased expenses. And as always when disaster strikes, those without a strong financial literacy foundation were the hardest hit.

For the financially literate, the pandemic was a challenging time but not necessarily a disaster. They had the tools and knowledge to adapt their financial plans, to find new income streams or to tap into their savings to weather the storm. They knew how to navigate the various government relief packages and how to negotiate with creditors. In contrast, those without this knowledge found themselves overwhelmed and unable to make the best decisions for their circumstances.

The COVID-19 pandemic has served as a stark reminder of the importance of financial literacy. The ability to manage one's finances is a crucial survival tool in unprecedented times. As we move forward and rebuild post-pandemic, we need to ensure that every American has this tool at their disposal.

Count Up the Costs

Financial literacy influences our daily decisions and shapes the course of our financial lives. Without it, we make choices that may seem harmless or even beneficial in the short term but are detrimental in the long run. Let's look at an all-too-common misstep: uninformed spending without thinking about the future.

We live in a culture of immediate gratification where we think of the "now" and don't have full appreciation for the future. When important financial life decisions are ahead, we often have a habit of punting the responsibility until later. The thing is that this type of thinking is a trap. We don't have as much time as we think. But this is no cause for alarm. It's simply a call to action.

Being an informed consumer helps us understand the tools that we need to build the lives we want at this very moment. Every dollar spent is an investment in our own gratification—either now or later. Without a secure grasp on the numbers, it's too easy to find ourselves spending money on things we don't need, with money we don't have on things that don't matter, to impress people we don't even know.

Now, let's talk about retirement. Traditional pensions are almost a thing of the past, and Social Security is often not enough to maintain a comfortable standard of living. And it's only going to get worse. According to the Social Security Administration itself, in just over a decade, they will only be able to pay out 75% of scheduled benefits.

There is no one else we can rely on to ensure our financial security in our golden years. It's on us, and sadly, we're not doing a great job. A study by the National Institute on Retirement Security found that nearly two-thirds of working millennials have nothing—nothing!—saved for retirement. As alarming as this is, it's not surprising given the current state of financial literacy. I wonder what Social Security payments will be when that generation starts to retire in about 30 years. I'm not optimistic about it.

Here's my point: Every dollar spent on nonessential items is a dollar not saved, not invested, and not available for unexpected (or expected) expenses later on.

Savings provide capital for businesses to invest and grow. Investments, especially in the stock market, help companies to expand, create jobs, and stimulate economic growth. When you know how to save, you can start to build wealth, to participate fully in the free enterprise system, and to play a role in fostering a healthier, more prosperous economy for everyone.

But by no means do I think we should stop enjoying life and become misers. No! The key is balance. How can we strike a balance between spending and saving? How can we make informed decisions that align with our financial goals? Well, first, we need to have financial goals! And then, we need to have an understanding of what it will take to achieve them. And for that, we need a basic understanding of how money works, when it's working for you, and when you're just working for it. And for that, we need widespread, easily accessible financial education for all.

Personal Accountability

Now, you may be asking about the role of personal accountability in all of this. And yes, personal accountability is important. We often say, "You can lead a horse to water, but you can't make it drink." That phrase rings true in many aspects of life, including financial literacy. Every individual must show initiative and take charge when it comes to their own finances.

However, it's equally vital to acknowledge the deeply rooted systemic barriers many communities face and that hinder their ability to take charge of their financial lives. Consider the psychological and mental toll that slavery, segregation, and ongoing systemic racism have imprinted on the minds of many Black Americans. This burden, often intangible and underestimated, can manifest as distrust toward financial institutions, skepticism about the attainability of the "American Dreams," and more tangibly, a lack of generational wealth to even begin the journey.

The many immigrant communities in America are not suffering from a lack of desire or ambition. They came to the United States for the specific purpose of pursuing the American Dream, for the freedom to control their destinies. It's only when they get here that they realize the myth of meritocracy; that they're starting several rungs down the aspirational ladder from the privileged classes; and that the color of their skin, the language they speak at home, and the lack of resources they arrived with make them invisible. There's no one teaching them how to navigate the system much less make it work for them.

And let's not forget the sections of the population who actively sabotage any chance of financial progress these groups are working so hard to make. Misled by popular misconceptions, they think that financial stability is a zero-sum game with winners and losers, and they want to make sure their kind wins.

While personal responsibility is crucial—you won't win in America without it—we also need to understand that for many, the starting line isn't the same. Not all have been given the same set of tools, resources, or even foundational knowledge to embark on this financial journey.

Only when these gaps are recognized and bridged can we truly boast of a society where everyone has not just the right, but the genuine opportunity, to financial freedom and success. As we forge this new era, we need to ensure everyone gets to see, understand, and climb that aspirational ladder.

Yes, It's Your Problem Too

If you're in a comfortable financial situation, you might be thinking: Yes, financial literacy is a problem for those less fortunate, but it's not my problem. And you'd be incorrect. The repercussions of a financially uneducated population, of even just segments of a population, go beyond individual or community bounds. They affect us all.

From high-earning families living paycheck to paycheck, to stress-fueled workplaces, to whole generations navigating their financial lives like boats without rudders, the evidence is clear. The lack of financial literacy is not a fringe issue. It is not a "them" problem; it's an "us" problem. Whether you're earning more than $250K a year or just scraping by, the ability—or inability—to effectively manage money, make informed decisions, and plan for the future has profound implications.

Stress and anxiety over financial matters can lead to reduced productivity, absenteeism, and even health issues. The cost of financial stress on the US economy runs into the billions of dollars each year.

And what about the fate of the future generations who will drive the economy? Fewer people have the financial resources or tools to navigate the college admission system, effectively closing off this avenue of economic advancement to them. Meanwhile, we are churning out graduates saddled with enormous debt and scant financial knowledge. The truth is that an increase in financial literacy isn't just about individual success stories; it's about fueling economic growth, increasing participation, and crafting a society where prosperity is a shared experience, not the exclusive domain of a privileged few.

Financial literacy is a crucial component of our nation's economic health and stability. So, as we move forward, we are going to explore how we can break this cycle of financial ignorance. How can we ensure that our young people are equipped with the knowledge and skills they need to make informed financial decisions? And most importantly, how can we ensure that all Americans, regardless of their socioeconomic background, can fully participate in our economy?

Empowerment Through Education

To truly renew America, we must inspire every community to aspire for better and perspire to make it happen. Yet, aspiration without a clear metric is like sailing without a compass. We might have the wind in our sails, but we'd be adrift without direction. We need the dream—education, entrepreneurship, and community engagement that leads to financial freedom for all—and we also need a plan: Empowerment Through Education. This is my upgraded business plan for America.

Breaking the Chains: From Fast Money to Lasting Legacy

Pop culture has an undeniable influence on the masses. Its catchphrases, values, and ideals infiltrate everyday life, shaping our thoughts, decisions, and desires. One such prevailing sentiment, particularly among the youth, is the notion of "getting to the bag"—a phrase that encapsulates the urgency of securing wealth rapidly, often without regard to the means or the future.

To many, especially in urban contexts, this "bag" symbolizes triumph over adversity, a tangible proof of escaping systemic constraints. Yet, the route to it often emphasizes short-term gains: quick money from fleeting trends, immediate gratification from luxury goods, and an overarching "live fast, die young" attitude. While the allure is undeniable, this perspective, when left unchecked, can be detrimental.

Growing up in Compton, California, and witnessing the birth and growth of hip-hop, I understand that the allure of fast money permeates not just in lyrics or screen dialogues, but manifests in real-world decisions. Immediate gratification drives many to spend beyond their means, to showcase a facade of success without the stability that should underpin it. This mindset not only perpetuates a cycle of debt and financial instability but also fosters a culture where future planning and wealth creation are overshadowed by the allure of instant rewards.

But this isn't an indictment of pop culture. It's a call to understand its nuances and direct its influence for positive change. The beauty of pop culture is its fluidity—it can evolve, inspire, and lead.

So, let's reframe the narrative.

Instead of "chasing the bag," imagine a world where the "bag" chases us—a world where passive income, investments, and generational wealth are the norms. The idea isn't farfetched; it's rooted in financial literacy. While bills might be settled by the toil of today, true wealth—the kind that impacts generations—is often cultivated in the strategic decisions that bear fruit over time, sometimes even while we sleep.

Financial literacy plays a pivotal role here. It offers the tools and knowledge to transform one's relationship with money. Through it, individuals can understand the power of investments, the magic of compound interest, and the importance of savings. They can navigate the complex world of credits and debits with confidence, ensuring they're not just earners, but wealth creators.

Data have shown the power of early financial education. A study by the National Endowment for Financial Education found that young adults who had taken a financial literacy course in school were more likely to budget, save, and invest wisely than those who hadn't. It's clear evidence that education can pivot the trajectory from "living for the day" to "planning for tomorrow."

Let's be clear: There's nothing inherently wrong with wanting the "bag" or the successes it symbolizes. But if we're truly committed to breaking chains, the journey must transcend momentary pleasures. It must be about creating legacies—lasting wealth that benefits not just the individual, but families, communities, and future generations.

In the end, the real power doesn't lie in the "bag." It lies in the knowledge, choices, and actions that determine whether that "bag" is a fleeting trophy or a foundation for a legacy. And it starts with educating our kids, our communities, our changemakers, and our workforce.

Educating Our Kids

Our traditional education system has mostly sidestepped the subject of financial literacy, leaving vast swaths of our youth unprepared for the challenges of the modern world. This makes the call to embed financial education in every school and in every community in America more than just a suggestion—it makes it a pressing necessity.

As we look around, financial decisions dictate much of our daily life. From credit card choices to student loans, and mortgages to retirement plans, the stakes are high. It's not just about numbers and interest rates. It's about life decisions, dreams, and aspirations. Financial literacy empowers individuals, offering them the agency to navigate an increasingly complex financial landscape.

But where do most of us learn about finances? Often, it's from our families. For those fortunate to have financially savvy parents, this education starts at home. But for many, especially in marginalized communities, such teachings are sparse, leading to generational cycles of financial disempowerment.

Unfortunately, when it comes to financial literacy, we are the product of our environment. Studies have shown that financial behaviors and beliefs are often passed down from generation to generation. We learn about money mostly from our parents and guardians, for better or for worse, reported the journal *Family Perspectives* in a 2022 academic review titled, "Financial Literacy: From Parent to Child," by Emilynn Jarvis Bleazard.

It's a domino effect. A child who grows up in a household where money is a constant source of stress, where bills pile up and debt is the norm, is likely to carry these habits and attitudes into adulthood. Without a solid foundation of financial education, that child may not understand how to break the cycle of living paycheck to paycheck, accumulating debt, or making poor financial decisions.

What's more concerning is what happens to their future children who unwittingly continue the pattern. We're effectively graduating generations of financially illiterate young people who grow up to become financially illiterate parents. This cycle of financial illiteracy is a significant contributor to the widening wealth gap and the perpetuation of economic inequality.

Schools have often been touted as the solution to this issue but, so far, are an untapped one. The reality is that most American students graduate high school without receiving any formal financial education. The current education system focuses on core subjects like math, science, and language arts, but financial literacy—an equally crucial life skill—is largely left out.

This systemic failing is leaving our youth ill-equipped to navigate the complex world of personal finance. They enter adulthood lacking the tools and knowledge to make wise financial decisions and often fall into the same traps their parents did.

Breaking this generational cycle requires a shift in our approach to financial education. Only then can we hope to equip the next generation with the financial skills they need to build wealth and secure their—and America's—financial future.

Financial Ed in Schools

Schools have always been a beacon of transformation, the great leveler. Financial education in schools can democratize access to knowledge, ensuring that every child, regardless of their socioeconomic background, has a fighting chance in the world of money.

But it needs to go beyond just theory. Kids need a practical financial education, one that integrates real-world financial situations into the curriculum. We need to equip them with the foundational knowledge to make informed decisions. We need to present budgeting, understanding credit, savings strategies, and even the basics of investments as more than concepts. We need kids to understand that these are tools for life.

So, while textbooks can provide the foundation, we need experiential learning to truly drive the message home. Schools can collaborate with local banks and financial institutions to organize field trips, inviting professionals to offer hands-on workshops. Hey, it worked for me! Such initiatives can demystify the world of finance, transforming it from a realm of intimidation to one of empowerment.

Imagine a high school program where students manage a mock investment portfolio and compete with other schools. Or a classroom simulation where kids are allocated a "salary" and need to budget their monthly expenses, to learn the consequences of overspending or the benefits of saving. That's what I'm talking about.

That's what will turn students into savvy consumers, entrepreneurs, and wealth builders. That's what will reduce their susceptibility to scams and predatory lending. That's what will keep their credit scores in the 700+ range and set them up to create the next generation of savvy consumers, entrepreneurs, and wealth builders.

Economic growth provides jobs, increases wages, and leads to a higher standard of living for its citizens. However, the engine for economic growth is not simply having more businesses or more products. It is the increased participation of the people within the economy. The more people are involved in economic activities, such as earning, spending, saving, and investing, the more robust the economy becomes.

This is why financial education is a lifeline in our modern world. And while the initial integration into our school system will require resources, training, and time, the return on investment—for our children, our communities, and our nation—is immeasurable. By committing to this path, we are not just teaching our children about money; we're equipping them with the tools to build brighter, more stable futures.

STEM (science, technology, engineering, mathematics) education is another area that requires an upgraded plan. STEM fields are at the forefront of innovation and economic growth today. They are the sectors creating the jobs of the future, jobs that promise not just a paycheck, but the potential for career progression and economic mobility.

Currently, low-income communities are significantly underrepresented in STEM fields, which has perpetuated a cycle of inequality. This is particularly concerning given that researchers from OpenAI and the University of Pennsylvania believe that by 2025, 80% of all jobs will require a certain level of technical proficiency. And the problem isn't getting better. Access to quality STEM education remains unevenly distributed, with schools in underprivileged communities lacking the resources to provide robust STEM programming.

To disrupt this cycle, we need to emphasize the importance of STEM education and ensure that it is accessible to all. This includes implementing effective STEM programs in schools, providing educators with the resources they need to teach STEM subjects effectively, and fostering an environment that encourages curiosity and exploration. Additionally, we must work to dismantle the systemic barriers that prevent minority students from pursuing careers in STEM.

STEM education isn't just about producing the next generation of engineers, scientists, or tech entrepreneurs. It's about equipping individuals with the skills they need to navigate our increasingly digital world and, in turn, empowering them to take control of their financial futures.

It Takes a Village

There's a saying I resonate with: "It takes a village to raise a child."

If you pause to ponder its essence, the message extends far beyond child-rearing. It captures the symbiotic relationship that binds us all together. We aren't just isolated islands; we're interwoven threads in this fabric called society. And this mutual reliance is most palpable when we talk about shaping financial narratives.

You see, too often, we place the onus of financial wellness on the individual. We over-index on personal responsibility while overlooking the important role of the community in lifting up our children. If you've ever found solace in a neighbor's advice, received assistance from a local organization, or simply drawn strength from your community's collective spirit, you understand this dynamic.

Communities flourish when local businesses thrive. They create jobs, circulate money within the community, and often provide products or services tailored to the unique needs of their neighbors. More than that, local entrepreneurs become role models, showing the next generation that success is achievable, and that their dreams too are valid.

This isn't just about wealth creation; it's about wealth circulation. When a dollar is spent in a locally owned business, it multiplies in value as it gets re-spent in the same community. This "multiplier effect" can be significantly higher for local businesses compared to chains or outside enterprises.

History is brimming with instances of communities rallying together in the face of adversity. When economies went through upheavals or when systems failed the ordinary person, it was communities that became the first responders. They provided safety nets, pooled resources, shared wisdom, and most importantly, instilled hope.

Now, juxtapose this community strength with the complexities of our financial landscape. In an era of instant transactions, digital currencies, and global economies, it's easy to feel lost or overwhelmed. But here's the thing: While the tools and systems evolve, the underlying principles remain rooted in the timeless values of trust, collaboration, and shared growth. And it's in our communities where these values truly come alive.

Think about your community's role in your financial life. Remember that elderly couple who first taught you the value of saving? Or that local business owner who gave you your first job, no questions asked? These seemingly minor interactions play a monumental role in shaping our financial psyche. Remember, real change, the kind that's lasting and profound, doesn't just come from the top. It bubbles up from our communities. It's time we acknowledge, celebrate, and harness this power. I discuss one way next.

Child Savings Accounts

When we look at our children, we often see a canvas of possibilities. A bright, boundless future waiting to be shaped by their dreams and aspirations. Yet, as any painter will tell you, a canvas, no matter how beautiful, needs the right colors to come alive. In the case of our children, these colors are the resources, the opportunities, and the platforms we provide them. One essential resource is financial security, and this is where Child Savings Accounts (CSAs) come into play. A CSA is an investment in a child's future. It's more than just a bank account; it's a commitment to their dreams, a vote of confidence in their potential, and a tool to teach them the power of savings and investments.

Operation HOPE and Atlanta Public Schools recently launched the HOPE Child Savings Account Program. Every kindergartener in the school system who attends a Title One school receives $50 to help launch their financial futures. The families and communities of these students will have the opportunity to contribute annually up until their senior year of high school. Upon graduation, students will have grown a healthy fund as a launchpad to help further their education or make a major investment into their life and futures. All from the seed fund back when they were five of $50.

A child can have a savings account opened for them at birth. The earlier, the better (remember the magic of compounding?) because they are designed to provide long-term savings for children. All you need is one small initial deposit to begin. Future contributions can come from parents, friends, family, community members, and even the children themselves as they grow older.

Now, you might be wondering, "Why not just open a regular savings account?"

Here's the key difference: CSAs are often paired with financial education. They serve as real-life platforms for children to learn about managing money, understanding interest, and making informed financial decisions.

They also have a deeper, more profound impact on the financial trajectory of kids, on their hope for their future. Studies have found that children with CSAs are more likely to attend college and less likely to accumulate debt in adulthood. They're more likely to believe in their future, to visualize their dreams, and to realize that they're within their grasp. In fact, the Children and Youth Services Review published a study in 2013 that found that low-income children with $500 or less in a savings account dedicated to college are three times more likely to go to college and four times more likely to graduate than their peers without dedicated savings.

By investing in CSAs, we're creating a safety net for our children. We're instilling in them the confidence to chase their dreams. And we're creating a financially literate and empowered generation that's ready to take the reins of their financial destiny and steer it toward prosperity.

CSAs also contribute to community growth and societal progress. In fact, the success of CSAs is highly contingent on community engagement. Many successful CSA programs, such as the SEED for Oklahoma Kids (SEED OK) experiment, have been backed by community initiatives and public policy interventions.

When communities come together to invest in their children's futures, they're fostering a culture of financial empowerment and resilience. This sense of collective responsibility and shared commitment creates a powerful ripple effect.

Consider this: A child, armed with the knowledge of personal finance and the cushion of a savings account, grows up to be a financially responsible adult. They're less likely to be burdened by debt, more likely to invest wisely, and more capable of weathering financial storms. This financial stability isn't just personal—it extends to their families, contributing to a more resilient community fabric.

The US Government Accountability Office conducted a study showing that children with CSAs are also more likely to pursue higher education, leading to a better-educated workforce that can better drive local economic growth. They're also likely to pass on their financial knowledge and habits to their children, creating a virtuous cycle of financial literacy and empowerment.

And let's not forget that very important psychological aspect. A CSA is a powerful message to a child. It tells children that their community believes in them, invests in them, and is rooting for them. This vote of confidence can boost their self-esteem and aspirations, which in turn, can have a positive impact on their academic performance and overall life outcomes.

Ultimately, the CSA is not just a policy tool or a financial instrument. It's a symbol of hope, a beacon of support, and a testament to the power of collective action.

By fostering CSAs, we're not just nurturing our children's dreams—we're building stronger, more resilient communities, one child at a time.

Educating Our Communities

To effect significant change, it's crucial that our approach to financial education be as inclusive and accessible as possible. This means delivering curricula in a way that meets communities of people where they are in terms of their unique needs, circumstances, and levels of understanding.

Everyone's financial journey is different. The challenges faced by a single parent working two jobs to make ends meet are vastly different from those faced by a young graduate just starting out. Likewise, the financial knowledge required by a small business owner may differ greatly from that of a retiree. To be effective, community-based financial education needs to take these different scenarios into account. It needs to be tailored to the realities of its audience.

So how can we achieve this? One approach is through differentiated learning—that is, providing different people with different learning pathways based on their specific needs. For instance, a small business owner may need information about managing cash flow and securing funding, while a young graduate may need advice on managing student loan debt and saving for the future.

Technology can also play a vital role in making financial education more accessible. With online learning platforms, we can offer personalized learning experiences at scale. Users can learn at their own pace, in their own time, and in a way that aligns with their specific needs. Digital tools can make learning more interactive and engaging. Whether it's through budgeting apps, interactive quizzes, or online simulations, technology can bring financial concepts to life in a way that's both fun and effective.

But making financial education more accessible isn't just about breaking down barriers; it's about meeting people where they are. It's about understanding their unique needs and circumstances and delivering education in a way that resonates with them. Courses should be offered at convenient times and locations, and online learning options should also be available. To ensure everyone can participate, training should be affordable, if not free.

Of course, differentiated, technology-driven learning solutions require significant resources. That's where private corporations come in. We have to get more private corporations to step up to support the communities they operate in. It's a beautiful thing. Their resources and innovation undeniably create tangible changes. Now imagine the magnitude of transformation we could create if their efforts were strategically aligned with public initiatives to spread financial literacy. By joining forces, these partnerships can create comprehensive financial literacy programs, outreach initiatives, and mentorship opportunities that are tailored to the unique needs of various communities, especially those that have been historically left out of the free enterprise system.

Public-private partnerships are not just about pooling resources, though that's reason enough to encourage them. They also create a sense of shared responsibility and mutual benefit. For the private sector, it's a chance to give back to the community and, in turn, foster goodwill that often translates into customer loyalty and brand equity. For the public sector, it's a cost-effective way to promote financial literacy and empowerment and, in the long term, reduce inequality and stimulate economic growth.

Let's talk specifics. What could a community-based financial literacy program look like? The government might provide a space—a local school or community center—and authorize the use of some resources to support the project. A private corporation, on the other hand, could offer funding, employees as volunteer instructors, and technological solutions to make the program accessible to more people.

One of the most effective ways to foster financial literacy and boost economic development within communities is through training and skill development. These initiatives can take many forms—from workshops teaching the basics of financial management to courses in entrepreneurial skills. What they all have in common is the potential to drastically improve the socioeconomic landscape of underserved communities. According to a report from the Jameel Poverty Action Lab, skills training programs have been shown to increase income and employment rates among participants. There's also a direct impact on individuals' attitudes and perceptions. When people see that they can improve their circumstances through learning, they're more likely to invest time in self-improvement and encourage others to do the same.

We're talking about collaboration at its finest, the kind that transcends the limitations of individual entities and allows us to make larger strides toward a financially literate society. I have seen firsthand, through my work with Operation HOPE, the powerful impact that public-private partnerships can have on communities. By merging resources, we've been able to provide essential financial literacy programs and services to those who need them the most. We've seen the profound, life-changing effects that these programs have on individuals, families, and communities.

So how do we encourage more of them? That's a conversation we need to have in our boardrooms, our government offices, and our communities. Let's start by promoting the value and impact of these partnerships, highlighting the success stories, and showing how they can be a win-win for everyone involved. Here's a story you can use to help the cause.

Case Study: The Singapore Model of Financial Education

Background

In the early 2000s, Singapore's government recognized the importance of financial literacy as a cornerstone for the nation's continued growth. However, they also acknowledged the limitations of public resources to single-handedly handle the challenge.

Action

In 2003, the Singapore government spearheaded a collaboration with private banks, insurance companies, and educational institutions called the MoneySENSE initiative. MoneySENSE was not just about teaching people how to save or invest; it sought to embed in Singaporeans a holistic understanding of money, of their rights as consumers, and of how the financial landscape works.

Implementation

The MoneySENSE initiative focused on four areas:

1. Curriculum: Major banks in Singapore offered both resources and personnel to craft a financial literacy

curriculum for schools. By 2010, financial literacy was seamlessly integrated into math lessons, civics classes, and more.

2. Community: MoneySENSE frequently organized roadshows in community centers around the island. These weren't just lectures but interactive events with games, quizzes, and prizes. Local banks, under the MoneySENSE banner, would set up booths offering free financial advice, workshops, and planning sessions.

3. Digital Outreach: Partnering with tech firms, MoneySENSE created online games and simulations targeted at younger audiences. These games, often tied to school competitions or national events, made learning about money fun and interactive.

4. Workforce Training: Recognizing that it's not just the youth that needed financial literacy, MoneySENSE collaborated with corporations to provide lunchtime financial learning sessions for employees. Experts from partnering banks and institutions would offer short courses that focused on a range of financial topics from retirement planning to property investment.

Outcome

Fast forward to today, and the results are clear. Singaporeans, on average, display a high level of financial literacy, according to a 2023 study on "The importance of financial literacy: Evidence from Singapore," published in the Journal of Financial Literacy and Wellbeing. The culture of savings, prudent investment, and financial planning is embedded in the society. While it's true that Singapore's size makes nationwide initiatives more manageable, the core principles of their success can be replicated on a larger scale. Their commitment to public-private collaboration, the blending of formal education with fun community initiatives, and a keen understanding of the target audience made all the difference.

Such examples should motivate us. If a small nation-state can achieve such significant strides in less than two decades, imagine the possibilities within our diverse and resource-rich country. The blueprint is there; it's up to us to customize it to our unique needs and challenges.

Taking a Cue from Singapore: A Story Worth Sharing

Now, you might be thinking, "John, what does Singapore, a tiny island nation, have to do with the massive complexities of the US financial system?" Well, hold on to your hats because this story is one for the books.

Back in the day, around the early 2000s, Singapore faced a dilemma. They saw the horizon, a future where their people needed to be savvy with their finances. But the government knew they couldn't do it alone. Here's where the magic happened.

Instead of going at it solo, the government joined hands with private banks, insurance bigwigs, and schools. They birthed this brilliant initiative called MoneySENSE. And no, it wasn't about making cents, but making SENSE of money.

Imagine this: Schools, with the backing of big banks, teaching kids not just math or history but how to manage their money, understand the power of investments, and knowing their rights as consumers. It was financial wisdom weaved into their daily lessons.

But they didn't stop there. They took to the streets—quite literally. Community centers buzzed with activity, with road-shows and events making learning about finances a community fest. And the young ones? They were playing online games crafted by tech giants, where saving coins in the virtual world meant understanding its value in the real one.

And here's the cherry on top: Corporations, from tech firms to food chains, had lunchtime money sessions. Employees, while munching on their sandwiches, got a dose of financial advice and planning.

Today, you walk down the streets of Singapore, and you see a society armed with financial wisdom. It's not just about the money; it's about the culture of making informed choices.

Now, America is no Singapore. We're vast, diverse, and complex. But stories like these show us the roadmap. If they can do it, so can we. It's about taking the initiative, fostering partnerships, and infusing financial wisdom at every level.

10

Educating Our Entrepreneurs

Entrepreneurship isn't just about starting a business—it's about embracing a mindset, one that is filled with resilience, innovation, and a relentless pursuit to turn visions into realities. Throughout history, the entrepreneurial spirit has been the driver of societal progression and innovation.

From the time I began my journey with Operation HOPE, I've been acutely aware of the transformative power of entrepreneurship. I've met countless individuals with burning ideas, immense talent, and an indomitable spirit. And yet, many of these brilliant minds face roadblocks—often systemic, sometimes circumstantial—that limit their potential. In the past, for marginalized communities, especially the Black community in America, these barriers have been insurmountable. But they don't have to stay that way.

From restricted access to capital and biases in lending, to a lack of financial education, business mentorship, and resources, Black and brown entrepreneurs often find themselves navigating a maze of challenges. We can bridge this gap by creating accessible funding for budding entrepreneurs, developing mentorship programs to help light the way, and providing training and skill development classes.

Funding Dreams

In the world of entrepreneurship, funding is the fuel that turns ideas into reality. Without it, even the most brilliant concepts remain just that—concepts. And for far too long, communities of color, particularly the Black community, have been deprived of this vital fuel. Creating accessible funding is about more than just providing capital. It's about trust, belief, and validation. It's about telling every would-be entrepreneur, "Your ideas matter. Your dreams are valid. And we believe in your potential to succeed."

Access to capital is more than just about money. It provides individuals the opportunity to dream, to innovate, and to create. But most importantly, it recognizes and validates the entrepreneurial spirit that exists in previously overlooked communities. This absence of access is not just a mere oversight; it's a systemic shortcoming that has stifled dreams and aspirations for generations. So, how do we rectify this? Here are some options.

Microfinancing: Traditional banking institutions often see small businesses and startups as risky investments, making it difficult for aspiring entrepreneurs to secure loans. Microfinancing can help fill this gap. Originating in Bangladesh with the founding of the Grameen Bank by Nobel Peace prize winner Muhammad Yunus, microfinance offers small loans to entrepreneurs who would otherwise be deemed "uncreditworthy" by traditional banking standards. By offering these small, low-interest loans, we can provide a lifeline to those who need it most. Plus, history has shown us that micro-loan repayment rates are often higher than traditional loans, dispelling the myth of risk associated with lending to low-income individuals.

Targeted Investing in Minority-Owned Businesses: By investing specifically in minority-owned businesses, we can stimulate economic growth in underserved communities. Not only can this create jobs and boost local economies, but it can also help rectify historical financial inequities.

Community-Based Funding Platforms: These platforms function on the principle of "community lending" or "peer-to-peer lending." By setting up local investment pools, we can encourage community members with a bit of extra money to invest in local businesses. This not only provides necessary funds but keeps the money within the community, further bolstering local economic development. Think of it as a communal piggy bank where individuals can borrow funds to start their businesses, and once they're successful, they replenish the pot, allowing others to do the same. This model makes capital more accessible and instills a sense of shared responsibility and mutual growth within the community.

Inspiring the Next Generation

Representation matters because it influences our perception of what's possible. When young people in marginalized communities see successful individuals who look like them in finance and business, it opens their minds to new possibilities. It breaks down the psychological barriers that limit their aspirations.

The current lack of minority representation in finance and entrepreneurship isn't just detrimental on an individual level. It's harmful to communities and the broader economy as well. Diversity fuels innovation, and when certain voices are missing from these spaces, we miss out on potential solutions and ideas. But we can change this. Role models can provide guidance, mentorship, and a tangible example of what success looks like. They're living proof that it's possible to overcome adversity and achieve financial success. And the role models are out there. We just need to be better at highlighting them. The more we share their stories, whether through local media, community events, or school presentations, the more impact they can have.

Mentors are a special category of role models who provide direct guidance, wisdom, and support. They help budding entrepreneurs navigate the tumultuous waters of the business world, sharing their experiences, knowledge, and network. They offer their experiences as learning opportunities, thus enabling mentees to avoid common pitfalls and navigate challenges more effectively. Within marginalized communities, the lack of mentorship often stems from the absence of accessible role models. Many individuals from these communities do not see themselves represented in successful entrepreneurial roles, leading to a (wrong) belief that these dreams are out of reach. By introducing mentorship programs, we can challenge this narrative and inspire a new generation of entrepreneurs.

Mentors and Building Relationship Capital

Role models and mentors can be entrepreneurs who've built successful businesses, financial professionals who've climbed the corporate ladder, or even educators who've devoted their careers to teaching financial literacy (smile). It's important to show that there's no one roadmap for success, to show that once you have the tools to succeed, you can create your own path.

Having a mentor can make all the difference in an entrepreneur's journey, providing them with the knowledge and confidence they need to succeed. They represented a game-changing experience in my life.

I didn't have an inheritance or generational wealth to lean on. I didn't have the benefit of wealthy or well-connected parents or someone in my family who could provide a key internship to me in an office complex in the neighboring city to the poor one where I lived. I didn't have a scholarship to a prestigious college, where I would meet hopefully lifetime friends and make professional relationships I could call upon. None of these represented resources, assets, or outlets available to the young man with big and bold aspirations that was me.

I knew that there was a business plan for success—I could see the manifestations of it everywhere in the outside world. I just never saw it operationalized with any consistency in my community. And so, I had to go find it myself. The bridge was the people in and around my life in the first instance (in my school, in my neighborhood and community), and later the people and leaders I sought out. I had to leverage the one form of capital I could access, something I now call relationship capital.

Growing up, my first mentors were people who were smarter and more connected than I was. I could learn from them and model their behavior, and perhaps, I could inspire them to believe in me. This included my father, Johnie Will Smith, who was a small business owner in South Central Los Angeles, and of course, my mother, Ms. Juanita Smith, who was a homemaker initially, and later on a tradeswoman and part-time small business owner.

Early on, my mentors included my elementary school principal and a couple of my teachers who listened to the bold dreams I had for myself, and who occasionally purchased whatever mail order items I was selling in the briefcase I had begun to carry around.

My mentors included that white banker who showed up in my fourth-grade classroom in Compton, California, and who famously taught me and a room full of nine-year-olds our first lessons in financial literacy. This lesson then led me to start my first business, the Neighborhood Candyhouse.

Needless to say, my life has been significantly influenced by mentors, and my interaction with every one of them delivered to me a fundamentally different "future asset value" in my evolution and learning process as a man. This is because all of them were and are vastly different like their own success and evolution in life. But it was all of interest to me. Remember, my primary education didn't come from a standard learning process, so the world became an open university for me. I saw "books of knowledge" everywhere.

One of my mentors and friends is Quincy Jones, the famed music producer, and when I asked him how he got so smart, he quickly responded that he was just "nosy as hell." He wanted to know everything about everything, and he told me that this was certainly also my trait. It still is to this day.

My mentor Tony Ressler taught me that you make money during the day, but you build wealth in your sleep. It compounds when you sleep. The overnight compounding effect for me is all the knowledge capital that I secured from my relationship capital, acquired throughout the entirety of my life.

Mentors and role models were everywhere in my life, mostly because I was always actively looking for them, everywhere that I was, and everywhere that I went.

My father was a mentor for hard work.

My mother was a mentor for unconditional love. She told me she loved me every day of my life. That alone transformed me. Gave me the power of self-esteem.

There was Dave O'Meara, who owned Malibu Cinema in Malibu, California, and who was an early believer in me. I don't remember where he and I first met, but I was committed to making sure that he would never forget about me. And he never did. I would go to meet him at his cinema after I finished working at the local mini-mart evening shift, and we would just talk about life, his and my own. And I would learn everything I could from him, about how he ran his small business. After a while, he started asking me other questions, like "What can I do to help you with your dreams?" That led to me writing a quick business plan, for what would end up being a half dozen mini-business ideas I tried, and Dave helped to finance. I even purchased a car from Dave to help me get around and pursue my evolving business ideas. Unfortunately, my mini-investment ideas that Dave backed didn't work out, but our friendship and his belief in me did.

Dave introduced me to my next mentor, of sorts, whose name was Stephen Cotter Miller. Dave introduced me to Steve because it was time for me to try to pay back some of the money I had borrowed, and Dave believed that I would only be able to do that by having a job. Steve was chairman of Wade, Cotter & Co., a local investment banking firm. Of course, I knew absolutely nothing about banking. But that didn't stop Dave or Steve, and later, me. And this just shows the undeniable power of relationship capital. I knew nothing about high finance or banking or investment, and respectfully, back then I didn't know I had an interest.

You can read some of my other earlier books to get the exact story of this period of my life, but the gist is that without these particular events, without the accident of one mentor introducing me to another (because I owed the first one money and he wanted to be paid back), I would have likely never founded Operation HOPE and engaged in a career rooted in finance and real estate.

And there was Dr. Cecil "Chip" Murray and Bishop Charles E. Blake, two prominent African American men of faith and leaders in the community of South Los Angeles. From them I learned how to live a life of steady character and how to be what I call today "an honest brother" so that the community, and those within it, trust and believe in you. They taught me that certain things were just not for sale. Like my soul. My consciousness. My core values. My belief system. My "what I'm for." I learned from men like these two, and they also protected me. They protected me from unscrupulous and jealous politicians and anyone else who saw what I was doing (and building) as a threat to them. Because of men like these, my dreams were given free reign.

There was William Hanna, who was then chief executive officer (CEO) of Cedars Bank, which was our first banker for Operation HOPE. He spent time with me, believed in me, and gave me my first business line of credit, which was $25,000 for the entire organization. The government shut down around the same time, and we very quickly tapped all of that original credit line and needed $75K more. I went to William Hanna, not as a banking client, but through the personal relationship capital we had built up together. And it worked. He extended the additional credit we needed, on my word—because the organization's balance sheet certainly could not and would not have justified it. By the way, this also shows the power and importance of small community banks, as a large institutional money center bank, as they are called today, simply could not have made this decision to give me the credit I needed on my word alone. That's some financial education right there.

Since then, there have been way too many mentors and role models and influencers in my life to mention them all, but here are a few more standouts. Dr. Dorothy I. Height, of the National

Council of Negro Women. Moral and civil rights leaders like Rev. C.T. Vivian, and of course my personal hero Rev. Andrew Young. Bank CEOs like Bill Rogers and Bryan Jordan. High-level executives and professionals like Tim Welsh and Steve Ryan, Esq. and successful entrepreneurs like Harvey Baskin, and so many more.

This group and others comprised my open university and my ride-or-die posse of supporters, backers, and believers. And so, one thing is clear in my life, and that is I am me because others believed in me, mentored me, gave me their time and attention. They listened to me. They didn't always agree with me, and sometimes they had to turn me down or turn me away—but the power of listening, and being heard, is in itself a significant value.

Now, I try to pay it forward to a new generation of young leaders making it in the world today. That's precisely why as CEO of Operation HOPE and several other growing organizations, I still make time every day to respond to comments on social media, and we publish a hopefully inspiring (and educational) video just about daily. The method of sharing the message has changed, but the substance, meaning, and reasoning behind those messages remain the same. Lifting people up. Just like I was lifted up.

The book *The Tipping Point* by Malcolm Gladwell makes a powerful point about role models. Citing a University of Illinois study, it showed that with just 5% of positive role models, a community stabilizes. What struck me here, is that it wasn't 70% role models, or even 50% cited. It wasn't 40% or even the 20% that followed Dr. Martin Luther King, Jr.'s civil rights movement. (It has widely been reported that Dr. King only enjoyed 20% of the white or Black community's support, at the height of his movement work, and yet it was transformational and had historical ramifications that we still feel to this day.) The magical number here, was simply 5%.

At 5% role models, the study found, every community stabilized. This is mind-blowingly powerful—and achievable, even by the most cynical standards.

First, we need to ensure that mentors are representative of the communities they serve, that they have faced similar challenges, and have real-life insight into how to navigate them.

Second, the program should be designed to foster long-lasting, meaningful connections between mentors and mentees. Quick, one-off sessions, while beneficial, cannot provide the depth of knowledge and guidance that ongoing relationships can.

Last, mentorship programs should be accessible. Whether it's through community centers, online platforms, or local events, these programs should be easy to find and easy to join.

Mentorship programs have the power to transform communities by fostering entrepreneurial success. By investing time and resources into these programs, we can ensure a more equitable future where everyone, irrespective of their background, has the chance to succeed.

Through these initiatives, we can democratize entrepreneurship, making it a viable and accessible path to financial independence for all.

11

Educating Our Workforce

Not everyone has the desire to be an entrepreneur. And that's okay. A financial education and empowerment program must also cater to those who want to succeed in the modern workforce.

Financial freedom is not just about ensuring equal access to resources or leveling the playing field through policy and education. It's also about creating opportunities for people to develop the skills they need to climb whatever organizational ladder they have an eye on. On-the-job financial literacy skill development programs not only provide individuals with the skills they need to compete in the workforce but also empower them to take control of their financial futures.

Picture this: You walk into the human resources office of your new job, and there on the table is your employment package. You see the usual suspects—health insurance, dental, vacation time—but nestled among these typical offerings is something you didn't expect. Financial well-being benefits. Your employer isn't just interested in your physical health; they're committed to your financial health too.

This notion might seem a bit farfetched, but it shouldn't be. After all, financial well-being is a critical aspect of a person's overall health and well-being, and financial stress is a significant contributor to mental health problems. Why shouldn't financial well-being resources be as commonplace as health care resources in an employment benefits package?

Imagine having a financial counselor as part of your employment benefits, a personal guide who helps you with everything from understanding taxes to making savvy investment decisions. But let's not stop there. What if your employer also offered financial literacy workshops, and regular sessions where everyone from interns to executives can come together to learn about the intricacies of personal finance—from retirement planning and understanding loans and mortgages to effective budgeting and so much more?

Now what if your company went a step further by creating incentives to use these financial wellness benefits? Matching contributions for retirement savings. A reward system for employees who complete financial education programs, and just as importantly, time off to attend sessions. A platform where employees can share their financial success stories. Feedback loops to ensure a dynamic and responsive learning environment that fits the needs of the workforce.

Everybody would win. Employees who are financially secure and not distracted by the stress of living paycheck to paycheck are likely to be more focused, more productive, and more committed to their work (because they know how to use their paycheck to secure their future).

And companies that show genuine care for their employees' well-being, including their financial health, can build a reputation as an employer of choice, attracting top talent in a competitive market.

Some forward-thinking companies are already leading this charge of employee financial wellness. These pioneers in corporate America are recognizing the profound impact financial literacy can have on their employees' lives and are doing something about it. PwC, for example, offers programs to help its employees pay off their student loans. And you'll learn more about Delta's highly successful financial wellness program, in partnership with Operation HOPE and Fidelity, later on in this chapter.

By reshaping their approach to employment benefits and making the financial well-being of employees a priority, these companies are creating a better-educated and more financially secure workforce. But these companies aren't just investing in their employees' financial futures; they are investing in the financial future of our nation. They are creating a culture of financial literacy because they realize that it is a necessary evolution for the modern workplace.

When employees become more financially literate and make smarter financial decisions, they contribute to a healthier economy. They become not just better workers, but also better consumers, better investors, and more informed citizens. The ripple effects can be far-reaching, extending well beyond the walls of the workplace.

What if your workplace was a hub of financial learning and empowerment, one where you have access to certified financial coaches, interactive financial education modules, and credit and money management workshops—all during your regular working hours? How would it feel to not have to navigate the confusing landscape of personal finance alone? To have experienced professionals and comprehensive resources right at your fingertips, empowering you to make informed decisions about your financial health?

Now what if I told you such a program already exists and is working its way into every major employer in the United States?

Operation HOPE's HOPE Inside the Workplace program was developed to bring financial empowerment and education directly to employees within their working environment. It is a program for integrating financial education and coaching right into the fabric of the workplace. More than just an added benefit or a one-off seminar, it's a full-fledged financial well-being program that is built into the employee experience.

We created HOPE Inside the Workplace to challenge the traditional boundaries of employee benefits and to enrich the working environment with the invaluable asset of financial education. In doing so, we are paving the way for a future where financial well-being is not just an aspiration, but an integral part of the work experience.

Yes, the framework and the programming already exist! The movement is already on its way.

The Delta Difference

Delta is more than an airline. It's also home to more than 90,000 employees, many of whose lives are defined by living from paycheck to paycheck. I first approached Delta about 2018, suggesting that they pilot our HOPE Inside the Workplace model. The CEO, Ed Bastian, and I were and are good friends, but I didn't want to tread on our friendship, so I went directly to their global human resources officer, Joanne Smith. Initially, Joanne didn't see what I saw, or she saw the kind of need through a different lens (we all need to get much more comfortable with folks seeing the world from a different lens and being okay with that). So I asked her for the next best thing: authorization to set Operation HOPE up somewhere within Delta, and see what comes. She graciously and kindly agreed.

It took two years and a crisis to bring the true value of financial literacy education into clear focus.

Sometime in early 2020, at the onset of the global COVID-19 crisis and unbeknownst to me, nervous workforce-level employees at Delta were heading to their respective 401K plan portals and requesting emergency withdrawals in overnight transactions. Quietly and without any fanfare or drama of any kind, more than $1 billion was withdrawn in emergency requests from Delta Airline employees retirement accounts! This number still shocks me.

No protests. No loud actions. No notice. Uncoordinated. Just folks sitting at their home computers in the middle of the night, in the desperate financial situation of needing to hit the "withdraw now" button. To Joanne Smith's credit, she called me and made it clear that the company now needed what we had to offer: financial wellness support for their employees. Within 30 days, the company committed to spread our HOPE Inside offices and HOPE financial coaches nationwide throughout their system. We began to make a difference, and in a town hall session for all Delta employees with me, Ed Bastian of Delta, and our friend Bill Rogers, CEO of Truist, Bill shared how he discovered a big financial problem that his bank employees had: Most didn't have even a few hundred dollars of their own for an emergency. To help support Truist employees, the bank decided to provide up to $750 to each employee who went through financial wellness coaching and counseling.

Ed Bastian is an outstanding leader for many reasons, and quickly identifying best-in-class practices is one of them. Not long after, Delta announced that it would provide $1,000 emergency savings accounts to each and every employee that went through our financial wellness coaching program (using either Operation HOPE or Fidelity, where their investment retirement accounts are managed). Ed, Joanne, and the team announced the enhanced program in January 2023 at their all-hands employee leadership session at Mercedes Benz Stadium. A team led by Kelley Elliot and others at Delta took the vision and drove it to the grassroots levels within the organization, touching everyone where they worked and operated. Online and in person. On the tarmac, if they had to. All we needed was a couple initial success stories, I believed, and success would take care of itself.

The company estimated that success could mean 20% of their employees signing up by end of the year. Within a month they met their original goal of 20%, and as of the time of this writing almost half of all Delta employees have finished the program and now have an emergency savings account that serves as a financial safety net in times of unscheduled challenges for themselves and their families. Here are some of the impressive top line results, as published on the Delta Financial Wellness website:

- 31,000 employees (almost 30% of its workforce) have enrolled in the program since January 2023.
- 21,500 Delta employees have already completed at least one financial learning track and had one coaching session, earning them $1,000 each from Delta to fund their rainy-day accounts.
- Participants have contributed an average of $1,061 of their own money to date—well above the required $250 contribution.
- Participants reported a 62% increase in their sense of financial control and a 139% increase in feeling able to save for other goals.

Today, the company views their financial well-being work with their 90,000 plus employees as one of two bookends of employee engagement support, in what I call a stakeholder capitalism model. On February 14, 2024, Ed Bastian announced more than $1.5 billion in employee profit-sharing bonuses. That's the other bookend: When the company does well, so do the employees. And when the company is experiencing challenges, like during COVID, the employees rally in support of the company and senior leadership. Delta didn't have to lay off one single employee during the pandemic, by the way. They all took a volunteer furlough, and they all came back when the world began to open back up in 2022. Today, Delta Airlines is the most profitable airline in the world, the most successful by market share and the most valuable by market value. That's not an accident. Success is intentional, and Delta and Ed smartly realized that their people are as important as their planes and on time schedules.

Elevating Credit Scores and Empowering Dreams

The United States of America, in many aspects, has lost its compass. We are grappling with meaningless divisions, fighting needless economic wars, and forgetting the shared dream that unites us all. Our salvation lies in uniting around a renewed vision for America—a vision driven by data and bound by the aspiration for financial dignity for every citizen.

Our nation, much like any thriving entity, needs a well-structured business plan. Not one rooted solely in rhetoric and lofty ideals, but one grounded in clear metrics, tangible goals, and outcomes. I believe that central to this new business plan for America is the HOPE Financial Wellness Index.

The HOPE Financial Wellness Index was created by me and my team at Operation HOPE and powered by Experian. This tool can provide a snapshot of a community's financial health as measured by the average credit scores of its residents.

At first glance, it's a tool, an index. But look closer, and it's a mirror reflecting the financial health and well-being of our neighborhoods. This index does not merely compile numbers; it marries resident credit scores with vital data on education, homeownership, income, life expectancy, and crime. It reveals the soul of our communities, making visible the invisible, and unmasking the true financial challenges and potential of neighborhoods across the United States.

I've hinted before at why credit scores are such an important indicator of financial health. Let me elaborate here. Credit scores don't just signal an individual's creditworthiness, they are an exceedingly precise barometer for the strength and resilience of entire communities. Raise a neighborhood's average credit score by just 100 points, and you'll witness a profound transformation—a decline in crime, the blossoming of families, and an overall uplifting in community wellness.

For example, we found that in 580 credit score communities, individuals live to around 61 years of age. It's important to note here that you don't collect Social Security until age 65. Now, just a mere 15 minutes away, in 700 credit score communities, people are living to 81 years or older. Think about that: A 120-point difference leads to 15+ more years of life.

In the 580 credit score community, most people have a high school degree, while in the 700 credit score community, they are college educated.

In the 580 community, you find a proliferation of single parent households (irrespective of race, by the way), while in the 700 community, it's overwhelmingly two-parent households.

In the 580 community, you have a very low homeownership rate—say 25% to 45%, while in the 700 credit score community it's more than 75%. And I don't care what anyone tells you, the easiest way to build wealth in America is still homeownership. Read that line back to yourself again for maximum impact please. Don't believe the hype. I'm telling it to you straight here.

Now where do you think all the crime, drugs, and depression is centered? Which community do you think attracts all the lowest rated fast-food restaurants? Don't trust me. Put this book aside, get in your car, and drive half an hour from most of your homes to an underserved area, be it Black, brown, and urban or poor, white, and rural, and you will see for yourself.

In fact, in the 580 community, the violent crime rate is 75 by 1,000 residents, while in the 700 community it's about 2 per 1,000 residents.

Nothing changes your life more, other than God or love, than moving your credit score 120 points. And that's what we at Operation HOPE are using the HOPE Financial Wellness Index to do. And that's why I sometimes refer to it as the HOPE 700 Credit Score Index—because a 700 credit score equates to financial well-being in America.

The HOPE Financial Wellness Index has mapped every zip code in America by credit score. Now, we're working with leading financial institutions to harness this data and translate it into tangible change. We are merging data-driven strategies with grassroots education initiatives to transform low credit score neighborhoods into beacons of financial well-being. Where once stood check cashers and payday lenders, we envision community-centric businesses, banks, and retail outlets that fortify the economic spine of neighborhoods. We are building a radical movement of common sense, at scale.

We are moving credit scores up 54 points in six months, moving debt down $3,800, and helping people to increase their savings by $1,100 on average. We are making people who earn $50,000 a year bankable. We are making it so that banks see them as valuable investments.

Consider this. Why would a bank say no to a loan or investment capital request for a person earning $50,000 a year? You may think they're being racist or biased, and on occasion they might be—but it also just might be that the person's credit score stinks, and his or her financial criteria is far from bank quality.

That person needs to upgrade his or her credit score and financial situation. If someone needs help, that's what we do every day at Operation HOPE. The education and support we provide has led banks and prime rate financial providers to unlock approximately $4 billion in capital flowing into underserved communities this way.

By raising the credit scores of communities, we are helping banks to get out of the "no business" (declining loans), and back into the "yes business" (investing in individuals and businesses) at scale because you cannot build or rebuild any community without having a dedicated banking sector and broad-based access to capital. This is our laser focus, and this is also our plan for the nation.

Approximately half of Black America has a credit score below 640, according to a 2021 survey from Credit Sesame. Not poor Blacks—I'm talking about college-educated folks and people walking around with suits and dresses and beautiful leased cars. Everyone. And while we may think our most serious problem is police abuse or the everyday racism we experience at a store retail counter, the truth is, this just might be worse—because every day half of Black America wakes up, pretty much 100% locked out of the free enterprise system. Let me be specific.

We cannot get auto loans with good rates and terms with a credit score under 640.

We cannot get a prime mortgage for the home of our dreams with a credit score under 680.

And we certainly aren't getting that loan to start that small business we've been dreaming about with a credit score below 700.

(FYI, unsecured small businesses are the highest risk credit extensions.)

But this I do know. If we can educate people on how to raise their credit scores from say 580 on average, to somewhere around 680 or better, we can stabilize America. I'm not willing this into truth. This is what the facts, the stats, and the data are telling all of us. Street by street. Neighborhood by neighborhood. Community by community. City by city and state by state—all boats will rise in line with their credit scores. Because the credit score is not only the best indicator of financial well-being, it's also the best indicator for some larger and even more important factors that we need to build a better America:

- *Optimism*
- *Hope and belief*
- *Well-being*
- *Self-esteem and confidence*
- *Trust and confidence in the financial system*
- *A sense of renewal and a plan for the future*

IV

It's a Movement,
Not a Moment

Empowerment Through Education is more than a push for policy changes or curriculum overhauls. It's a cry for a cultural shift, a change in the way we view and value financial education. Our message is a call to action for all Americans to join us in the fight for financial literacy, to share in our vision of a nation empowered, enlightened, and engaged in its financial future.

CHAPTER

13

Empowerment Through Education

If this book has illuminated anything, it's that financial literacy is not just a personal boon—it's a national imperative. But how do we communicate this imperative to the nation? How do we ensure that the urgency, the importance, and the sheer necessity of financial literacy reaches every household in America?

We have to harness their awareness. They can't do better until they know better. We have to make them aware of what they don't know.

What I know is this: It's not enough to implement public policies. We need to inspire individuals to embrace financial literacy for themselves *and* recognize the value that a financially educated population will have on their lives.

We have to get them excited about being part of something bigger, something life-changing, something nation-building. Every major societal shift has started with a handful of aware, driven individuals who dared to instigate change. We have more than a handful. Now it's time to get the rest of the nation in on the movement.

A movement begins with a whisper of discontent, a rumbling of unrest, and a spark of desire for something more. Eventually, this discontent, unrest, and desire coalesce into a unified message.

Messages are the heart of any movement. They carry the dreams, the desires, the goals, and the aspirations of a collective seeking change. Messages serve as the rallying cry, the banner that unites folks from different walks of life under a common cause. It's the hook, the headline, the tweet, the soundbite that draws attention, piques interest, and fuels the fire of collective action.

For our financial literacy movement, the message is simple yet profound: Empowerment Through Education. It highlights the direct connection between financial literacy and individual prosperity, community development, and national growth.

To make this message resonate, it needs to be omnipresent, embedded in our daily lives. It needs to echo in our classrooms, permeate our homes and communities, and reverberate through our workplaces. It needs to be a topic of discussion at the dinner table *and* barbershop *and* water cooler *and* playground, a part of our social media feeds, and a common thread that ties us all together, regardless of socioeconomic status, race, or credit score.

Making Financial Literacy "Cool"

Messaging about financial literacy typically comes from the top-down. The content and the methods of delivery are decided by those in the upper echelons of the institutions that play a significant role in our financial systems—banks, credit unions, investment firms, government bodies, and localized nonprofits. Each of these entities has mounted campaigns or initiatives designed to impart wisdom about financial literacy. While their intent has been good, there's been a disconnect that makes them ineffective.

The messages were crafted in corporate boardrooms, government offices, and well-funded nonprofits by individuals who did not share the same lived experiences as those at the receiving end of the communication. As a result, they were missing an essential element, which is alignment with the people who need this information the most.

Too often, the messaging around financial literacy is sterile, complicated, and detached from the realities of everyday life. It's designed to fit the molds of regulatory compliance or corporate responsibility, not the nuanced needs of various communities.

But when we talk about financial literacy, we shouldn't just be talking about understanding interest rates or retirement savings. We should be talking about managing day-to-day finances, navigating unexpected expenses, or working multiple jobs while trying to save for the future. About single parents trying to put food on the table, students saddled with college loans, families trapped in cycles of debt, and individuals trying to rebuild their lives after financial missteps.

For financial literacy messages to resonate, they must be culturally competent, tailored to the needs of the individuals, and delivered in a language they understand. We need to meet people where they are, not where we think they should be. This means going beyond the traditional mediums of delivery and embracing platforms where our target audience spends their time.

Because we're not just delivering information, we're fostering a movement. We're encouraging individuals to take control of their financial destinies. That means the messaging should not come as a directive but as a dialogue. We need to listen, understand, and respond to the questions, concerns, and experiences of those we aim to serve. We need to make financial literacy relatable, engaging, and empowering.

Financial literacy, I admit, doesn't sound as thrilling as the latest sports car or the newest tech gadget. Yet, the benefits it yields are far more enduring and impactful. And so we have to package this concept right.

Remember the ALS Ice Bucket Challenge that went viral a few years ago? It started as a simple fundraising initiative for Amyotrophic Lateral Sclerosis research and turned into a global phenomenon raising more than $115 million for the cause, largely because of its engaging, interactive nature and the enthusiastic endorsement of numerous celebrity figures.

Now, imagine if we could generate the same level of enthusiasm for financial literacy. What if we could turn learning about interest rates, budgeting, and credit scores into something as viral as the Ice Bucket Challenge?

America is the world capital of branding. Our brands have a knack for storytelling, making us connect with the brands we encounter and buying into their vision or corporate distinction. They can make a simple product or idea feel important, desirable, even *cool*. Why only limit the power of branding and marketing to building businesses? Why not leverage it for a cause as important as financial literacy and building each other up as we continue to build our nation?

We can create advertisements that make understanding compound interest as enticing as the latest smartphone. We can hire influencers on social media to promote the value of budgeting and saving as passionately as they do a new fashion line. We can even call on our leading-edge tech industry to develop a popular video game that subtly educates players about financial management. By aligning financial literacy with elements of pop culture and market trends, we can break down the barriers of complexity and tedium often associated with financial education.

We could even engage brands themselves in the movement. For example, a bank could offer special account perks to customers who complete a financial literacy course. Or a retail brand like Target or Walmart could offer discounts to customers who demonstrate savvy budgeting practices.

Standing on the shoulders of America's megabrands, we can make financial literacy "cool."

CHAPTER

14

Join the Movement

We've by no means exhausted the topic, but we have covered a lot.

We've talked about the problem, and we've laid out a solution—a multipronged approach that requires educational policy change, community engagement, partnering with US workplaces and financial institutions, and public awareness. And we need you.

Empowerment Through Education is a call to action. It is a plea for every person, every organization, and every institution to play their part in creating a financially literate society.

If you're a parent, start by teaching your children about money. Start a savings account for them and talk to them about the value of money to change lives. Teach them about budgeting and the importance of saving and investing.

If you're an employer, consider offering financial well-being programs to your employees. Foster an environment that encourages financial health, just as you would physical health.

If you're a part of a community organization, think about how you can incorporate financial literacy into your programs. Engage with organizations like Operation HOPE to bring financial education to the people who need it most.

If you're a policymaker or involved in government, use your platform to advocate for policies that promote financial education. Work toward embedding financial education in schools and creating partnerships that deliver resources to the underserved.

If you're a financial institution, rethink who you are serving. How are you delivering your messages, and who are they reaching? Partner with nonprofits, governments, and community organizations to bring financial literacy to the forefront.

And if you're someone from any community or sector of the population who has been inspired by this book, who sees the need for change, and wants to be part of it, join us. Join the Financial Literacy for All Movement. Be part of this national groundswell that works to communicate the importance of financial literacy.

Support the work of Operation HOPE by becoming a member of the 1865 Project—by becoming a paid member or volunteering your time as part of HOPE Corps or the HOPE Time Bank for projects like 1MBB (1 Million Black Business Initiative), and for those who want to provide more structured commitments of time to and for our work, we have the HOPE FILE (Fellows, Interns and Loaned Executives) Program.[i]

Because here's the thing, as clichéd as it may sound. We're all in this together. Financial illiteracy is not a problem for a few; it's a problem for us all. And. . .it's an opportunity for us all to build a more inclusive, equitable and prosperous society.

---

[i] In October, 2020, Shopify CEO Tobias Lutke and I announced 1 Million Black Businesses (1MBB), a 10-year initiative to create, grow, and scale one million Black-owned businesses. According to the U.S. Small Business Administration Office of Advocacy, Black-owned businesses make up only 10% (3.1 million) of all small businesses in the United States. In addition to this, only 3% of all Black businesses are job creators with the remaining 97% being sole proprietors.

Conclusion: A Ladder for All

In the global theater, where nations are continuously jostling for the number one spot as the leader of the free world, the United States stands as a beacon of democracy and freedom. A flawed beacon, but a beacon, nonetheless. But even as we hold our ground against external adversaries, we face internal pressures that threaten our unity.

Our greatest external competitor today is China, and it is actively capitalizing on these internal breaks, hoping to dislodge the United States from its place of influence. China's aspirations have never been so subtle and obvious at the same time. That's because its most strategic weapon isn't its industrial might or technological innovation; it's China's ability to perceive and exploit America's internal divisions. China's strategy to outdo America on the global stage entails ensuring we remain preoccupied with infighting and internal tumult. By fueling dissent and deepening divides, China is diluting our collective strength.

But here's the silver lining: *America has always emerged stronger from adversity*. The narrative of America is not one of an unbroken lineage of triumphs, but of resilience, of rising time and again from challenges. And the current situation, though daunting, is no different.

Each of us, regardless of background or belief, shares an intrinsic yearning for the American Dream—the promise of life, liberty, and the pursuit of happiness. This dream binds us; it provides a shared vision of hope and prosperity. But to actualize this dream in today's complex landscape, especially one that's riddled with systemic barriers for many groups, we need financial literacy for all.

At its core, financial literacy is about empowerment and control. In a world that seems increasingly chaotic, where news cycles are dominated by economic downturns, trade wars, armed conflicts, and financial uncertainties, being financially literate offers individuals a semblance of control, a shield against the unexpected, a tool to navigate the complexities of modern life.

Financial literacy transforms citizens from passive onlookers to active participants. When you don't know how to navigate the system that America runs on, it's all too easy to become pawns in a larger geopolitical game, to have your naivete manipulated for broader agendas. Financial skills and knowledge allow you to claim your agency, to go from pawn to player, from bystander to change-maker.

Embracing financial literacy is really about more than individual prosperity. It is a source of national unity and strength. A financially literate populace is less susceptible to divisive tactics. If you really understand the game, you know that playing to win means bringing everyone along with you. Because the true measure of America's success isn't in the heights reached by a select few, but in the collective rise of all our diverse communities.

Success in America isn't a zero-sum game, and one person's ascent doesn't mean another's descent. We need more than just individual communities or groups prospering in silos. We have that already, and it's not doing the trick. We need every demographic and section of our diverse society rising together. We need a society where individuals are not just focused on personal gain, but on collective growth.

Financial literacy is not just a checkbox to be marked off; it is a critical rung on the aspirational ladder of every American. Consider our Black and brown friends, the ones who have been made invisible, some for many centuries, but who are an integral part of the American tapestry. For them to fully invest in America's dream, they need to feel the grip of that rung in their hands. They need to be confident that it will support them on their ascent to financial stability and growth.

The same holds true for every community of every race in America: Asian, Middle Eastern, European, Latin-American, and African. They too must be able to discern this first rung on the ladder of aspiration, knowing that with every step they take, they're not only elevating themselves but contributing to the greater American narrative.

And let's specifically address this often-overlooked demographic: the poor and struggling white communities in America. Many from these communities once climbed, or at least aspired to climb, the ladder. Now, with the complexities of a globalized economy, shifting job markets, and social challenges, they have lost sight of what that first rung of the ladder even is. It might be a distant memory, but we can re-introduce to them this pathway for reclaiming their financial dignity.

Last, we cannot forget the backbone of our nation: the American middle class. They've long been emblematic of the American dream, the standard bearers of stability and progress. But now they see the ladder they once confidently scaled as brittle or broken. And in some ways, it is. That's why we're working to fix it. It's imperative for this vast demographic to witness a restoration of that ladder, not just for their sake, but as a beacon of hope for the future. We need them to know that the ladder can hold the weight of their, their children's, and their grandchildren's aspirations.

The world seems intent on highlighting and exploiting America's internal disparities, but not me. To me, the path forward is clear, and it is one of unity, underpinned by financial literacy. It is one of Empowerment Through Education. By arming our nation with financial literacy, we won't just stand undivided; we will be invincible against any force that seeks to challenge us.

I think we can change the world and fix our problems as a society and as a country. I think we can be truly great again, and that will come from us doing things *with* and for each other, not *to* each other. Hate never built anything. Love, hope, and a business plan does every day. And so, this book is our new business plan for America.

I see our so-called leaders tearing us apart with division—on both sides of the political aisle. I see folks pitting us against each other. That's precisely what countries like China and Russia want. They want us at war, cultural and political war, with each other. Because a house divided cannot stand (that's in the Bible by the way).

When we take our eye off the ball, our economy and economic miracle of a business model for a country, begins to sputter and die. And it's important to know this—there has never been a country that was leader of the free world that was not also, at the same time, an economic leader. These two things appear to go together.

So look at us. We are slowly falling apart. We are shooting ourselves in the collective foot. As someone once told me, "You can't take no pleasure that there is a hole in *my* end of *our* boat." We are all in the same boat, and we all need to be on the same page about fixing the holes. We need to have a collective vision for how we all will win.

And so, here's a vision for you that I believe can change everything for everyone, that can stabilize America.

The vision is moving credit scores 100 points, from community to community. No, that is not a typo, and yes, I am completely sober. I know exactly what I said (stop saying this guy must not be as bright as we thought he was and read it again). Because 700 credit score communities don't riot. Seven hundred credit score communities don't riot; they go shopping. Only 500 credit score communities riot. I'm joking, but I'm serious. Very. Think about this.

Some of my struggling friends say to me sometimes, "John, I really do hate rich people."

They are often surprised at my reply.

"No, you don't. You hate rich people until you become rich. What you hate is a gamed system. What you hate is a system that you believe is set against you, where the rules are not published, the playing field is not level, and where no matter how hard you work, nothing changes. You make no progress while watching others, seemingly much less intelligent than you, absolutely killing it at the game called life and success. That's what burns you up. But no worries—that's what I'm here for. That's what Operation HOPE is here for. A partner to help educate you on the rules of the game so you can win at life."

Empowerment Through Education: This is my business plan for America, and the star attraction, the leading asset in each example of change, and the CEO leading the charge and the change is you. Doesn't that give you hope?

Epilogue

My mother, Juanita Murray Smith, passed away on September 10, 2023, in Fayetteville, Georgia, but her legacy lives on, now in me. I'm a spiritual person, and so, quoting a prophet from long ago, I will tell you that I believe we are not human beings having a spiritual experience, but spiritual beings having a human experience.

Mom was a strong believer, and she loved the Lord. And this love for the Lord was with her even as a child when her dad died, and she and her sisters had to go to work as domestics to help make ends meet. Sadly, when she made $5 for a day's work, her mother—my grandmother—would take all of it and go gamble it away. Grandmother always thought that she could win big, but like most poor people, she never did. My mother learned that lesson, and one about savings and self-preservation too. After that, she would tell her mom that she only made $2.50 and saved the rest. That's a lesson in wealth building that would serve my mother well for life—always put something aside for yourself and your future.

But the first lesson my mother taught me, was about grit, resilience, and faith.

My mother was spiritual, but she didn't take any mess either when it came to her children—so she "dealt" with her then ex-husband's (the father of my two older siblings) abuse and prayed to God for an exit with her family from then East St. Louis. Enter my dad to be, who was making his way through East St. Louis on his way to purchase a new car in Detroit. Then he saw my mother, and everything (in his life and ours) changed.

My mother packed up her two kids, and my dad drove them all back to Los Angeles, where they built a life together and a small conglomerate, which included our own home, a gas station, an eight-unit apartment building, and a cement contracting business. And what a powerful pair. My dad could make the money, and my mother—because of the way she was raised—could save it. Unfortunately, my father never listened to my mother, and ultimately, they lost everything. Everything—100% of our generational wealth up until that point, including the $4,000 she had saved for my brother's college tuition. And so, my mother left my dad, once again packing her kids—this time all three of them (now including me).

There was my second lesson from my mother. A lesson about consistency, selflessness, financial literacy, and the power of saving.

My mother went to live with a friend to save money to buy her first home, which she purchased in Compton, California. I grew up in that house.

What I didn't realize then was that 15502 South Frailey Avenue was not just shelter; it was wealth building for the working single mother. It was access to equity, value appreciation, and real wealth creation. Mom went on to buy and sell seven homes, building equity that she would later use to fund down payments for first homes for my brother and sister.

The final business lesson from my mother came to me as a young man. Interestingly, it was the same one taught to me by my billionaire business partner and friend Tony Ressler later in my life:

> You make money during the day, but only build wealth during your sleep. It's called compounding.

This lesson is the gift that just keeps on giving. This is the wealth creation formula for the vast and vastly underserved—and for the struggling middle class who think that a steady paycheck is the route to a successful life.

Mom has been Promoted, now gone on to a better place, but boy did she make a magnificent difference while she was here amongst us, on this earth. And inside of me.

Every time I think about that $4,000 my mother saved for my brother, and the dreams it held, my heart aches a little. If only my father had known then, what I know now. The beauty of compounding. The power that lies in smart financial choices. The strength of tools like the Child Savings Account.

Remember, my best friend George and O.C., the man who saved my life? Both of them were murdered in front of me for not a lot of money. Imagine if they could see the world we're working to create now. A neighborhood where "chasing the bag" isn't the ultimate goal. Imagine if they had been able to be a part of a community that inspired (legal) entrepreneurship. Where smart isn't just encouraged; it's celebrated. The brilliance of George and the wisdom of O.C. could have thrived, creating legacies we'd all be proud of.

I've been talking a lot about reimagining the American Dream throughout this book. It's more than just a catchphrase. It's about leveling the playing field, making sure we're all getting a fair shot. No more elbows and shoves, but an open hand offering help to one another, a nation lifting each and every one of her citizens.

America has never been afraid of competition, both globally and domestically. But what if we competed with respect and equality? That's the America we aim for. A place where talents from everywhere want to be, not because of the glitz and glam, but because it's a land of real, tangible opportunity.

Lincoln, Douglass, King, and Young. Those names ring in our ears as a constant reminder of what could have been, what was lost, and what can be regained. They paved the way, did the work, and have contributed greatly to our world and society. Now, we're here to finish the mission: to take their dream of economic freedom for all and make it our everyday reality—every child armed with financial wisdom, every family sowing seeds of generational wealth, and every community embracing mutual respect and collective prosperity.

And so, even as I reflect on my journey and the journey of America, those early days, the struggles, the lessons, and the dreams, I continue to feel this surge of hope. Not just a fleeting kind, but one deep-rooted in belief. We're onto something special here.

The transformation of our nation? It's happening. Right here, right now, with each one of us playing a part. Let's remember, it's not just about investing dollars but investing in souls, in futures, in dreams.

We've come a long way, but the road ahead. . .that's the most exciting part. Every step we take, every choice we make, brings us closer to that shared vision. So, here's to America, to our journey toward truly equal opportunities for all. To the brighter, economically inclusive tomorrow we're building together. Let's keep the momentum going. After all, the best chapters are the ones we write together.

Financial Literacy Resources

There are a multitude of free online financial literacy resources available. Many of these are high-quality, meeting the standards set forth by leading financial literacy educators and researchers, and unbiased—meaning there are no strings attached, no catch, no product or service to buy offered right alongside the materials. That doesn't mean that financial literacy resources offered by financial institutions and other for-profit organizations, many of which are free, aren't high quality—it just means that you should be careful and think about the resource provider and whether they're more interested in selling you something rather than educating you.

Operation HOPE's Financial Literacy for All initiative (FL4A) believes in universal access to free, high-quality financial literacy information, tools, and resources, at every point in one's financial journey, and whatever the life stage, circumstances, need, or interest. We see this not simply as a "nice-to-have," but as a "must-have"—a civil right for this generation and beyond.

Listed next are several free online financial literacy resources provided by government or nonprofit organizations. You can also visit our online FL4A Resource Library, where we maintain a curated and continually evolving directory of free financial literary resources provided by government, nonprofit, and FL4A Member organizations at www.fl4a.org/resource-library.

The most important point to remember is this: When it comes to learning about personal finance, navigating financial challenges, and attending to one's financial future, there is *always* a free, high-quality resource available—always a place to turn for information, tools, resources, direction, and answers.

Visit FL4A's Resource Library, any of the sites listed here, your financial institution or another trusted entity, or do an online search. Whatever you do, use good judgment to make sure you're getting free advice that works *for you*, and *not for the provider*. And remember: The more you learn, the more you know, and the more you know, the better equipped you are to control your financial destiny and avoid financial predators.

Finally, for more information on national standards or "best practices" in financial literacy, we also provide links to a few notable resources.

Government Financial Literacy Resources

1. U.S. Department of the Treasury: Financial Literacy Education Commission (FLEC)—My Money: https://www.mymoney.gov/

2. US Office of the Comptroller of the Currency (OCC)—Financial Literacy Resource Directory: https://www.occ.gov/topics/consumers-and-communities/community-affairs/resource-directories/financial-literacy/index-financial-literacy-resource-directory.html

3. Federal Deposit Insurance Commission (FDIC—Money Smart:https://www.fdic.gov/resources/consumers/money-smart/

4. Consumer Financial Protection Bureau (CFPB): https://www.consumerfinance.gov/consumer-tools/, https://www.consumerfinance.gov/consumer-tools/educator-tools/, https://www.consumerfinance.gov/consumer-tools/educator-tools/library-resources/online-resources

5. Federal Trade Commission (FTC): https://consumer.ftc.gov/

6. National Credit Union Administration (NCUA): https://ncua.gov/consumers/financial-literacy-resources, https://mycreditunion.gov/

7. MyCreditUnion.gov: MyCreditUnion.gov

8. US Department of Defense (DOD) Office of Financial Readiness: https://finred.usalearning.gov/

9. US Federal Reserve Bank: https://www.federalreserve education.org/

10. US Department of Housing and Urban Development (HUD): https://www.hud.gov/counseling

11. US Securities and Exchange Commission (SEC): https://www.investor.gov/

12. New Jersey Department of the Treasury: https://njfinlit.enrich.org/

13. California Department of Education: https://www.cde.ca.gov/pd/ca/hs/finlitk12.asp

14. State of Georgia: https://consumered.georgia.gov/

15. Federal Reserve Bank of Dallas: https://www.dallasfed.org/-/media/microsites/cd/wealth/index.html?la=en&hash=CE80 DAC7B67AA1DADA5D6D8E17DF27B4

Nonprofit Financial Literacy Resources

1. Operation HOPE: https://operationhope.org/programs/

2. Operation HOPE Financial Wellness Index: https://operationhope.org/impact/financial-wellness-index/

3. Khan Academy: https://www.khanacademy.org/college-careers-more/financial-literacy

4. National Foundation for Credit Counseling: https://www.nfcc.org/online-courses/

5. Consumer Federation of America: https://americasaves.org/ and https://militarysaves.org/

6. Jump$tart Coalition—Financial Literacy Clearinghouse: https://jumpstartclearinghouse.org/

7. AARP: https://www.aarp.org/money/

8. FitMoney: https://www.fitmoney.org/

9. Junior Achievement: https://connect.ja.org/financial-literacy/

10. Next Gen Personal Finance: https://www.ngpf.org/, https://www.ngpf.org/arcade/

11. InCharge: https://www.incharge.org/financial-literacy/

12. American Savings Education Council: https://www.asec.org/services-5, https://www.asec.org/traps-and-pitfalls, https://www.asec.org/tools

13. Singleton Foundation for Financial Literacy & Entrepreneurship: https://singletonfoundation.org/programs/

14. Council for Economic Education: https://www.councilforeconed.org/programs/for-families/

Financial Literacy Resources—National Standards and Best Practices

1. Financial Literacy and Education Commission's (FLEC) National Strategy for Financial Education: https://home .treasury.gov/system/files/136/US-National-Strategy-Financial-Literacy-2020.pdf

2. Council for Economic Education (CEE) and Jump$tart Coalition: https://www.councilforeconed.org/policy-advocacy/ k-12-standards/

3. National Financial Educators Council (NFEC): https://www .financialeducatorscouncil.org/financial-literacy-standards/

Financial Literacy Checkup

1. Council for Economic Education (CEE): https://www .councilforeconed.org/personal-finance-quiz/

2. Financial Industry Regulatory Authority (FINRA): https:// www.finra.org/financial_literacy_quiz

3. National Endowment for Financial Education (NEFE): https://www.nefe.org/initiatives/NEFE-Life Values-Quiz-2021.pdf

The Financial Literacy for All Initiative

Christmastime, 2020. Operation HOPE founder, chairman, and CEO John Hope Bryant—a champion of financial literacy and empowerment of the underserved for more than three decades—called his friend, Walmart CEO Doug McMillon, with a notion:

"I think financial literacy should be the civil rights issue of this generation."

Doug's response?

"I agree. What are we going to do about it?"

We. "What are *we* going to do about it?"

Two of the most impactful people in the country.

Allied in recognition that a lack of financial literacy makes it extraordinarily difficult, if not impossible, for millions of Americans to make sense of their financial lives, putting the American Dream at risk not only for them but for their families and generations to come.

Bonded in the understanding that financial literacy is the cornerstone of any effort to disrupt poverty, alleviate financial struggle, and help everyone seeking to realize financial security and reach their potential.

United in their conviction that the time is *now* to make financial literacy a fundamental part of American life—and that the private sector is uniquely positioned with an opportunity, and responsibility, to help make this happen.

John and Doug jumped on the next step, immediately reaching out to Tony Ressler, cofounder and chairman of ARES Capital Management; Dan Schulman, founder, chairman and CEO Emeritus of PayPal; and seven other prominent CEOs from leading companies across the nation: Brian Moynihan of Bank of America, Ed Bastian of Delta, Bob Chapek of Disney, Sal Khan of Khan Academy, Adam Silver of the NBA, Roger Goodell of the NFL, and Rosalind Brewer of Walgreens Boots Alliance. In no time at all, there was a coalition of the willing: 11 companies committed from the top of the house to the life-changing mission of embedding financial literacy in our schools, workplaces, communities, and culture so that financial literacy becomes a reality for all and for good.

Formally launched through Operation HOPE in May 2021, Financial Literacy for All (FL4A) is a 10-year initiative to reach millions of youths and adults by meeting them wherever they are on their financial journey, ensuring they have access to and an understanding of the knowledge, tools, and resources they need to make informed financial decisions and take control of their financial lives. As of this writing, our coalition is nearly 50 members strong, collectively comprising more than a quarter of the companies listed on the Dow Jones Industrial Average and a combined employee and franchisee base of more than six million people. Our coalition is poised to grow, with plans to bring on more Fortune 500 companies and strategic-impact organizations, and ally with other leaders across the US who share common cause.

FL4A members are developing exciting, innovative programs and initiatives in support of our mission, making progress in our three core objectives:

- **Financial literacy for all students.** Requiring the inclusion of financial education at age-appropriate levels for K–12 and college students as part of the core curriculum, with appropriate alignment at the federal level.

- **Financial literacy for all adults.** Making comprehensive financial education, tools, and resources, provided by private sector, government, and nonprofit organizations, freely accessible to all adults and that meet each person wherever they are on their financial journey.

- **Amplify the mission and advocate for financial literacy.** Developing and implementing an ongoing campaign that highlights the critical importance and benefits of financial literacy for all, cementing it as "top of mind" in our cultural dialogue.

Each member has already made a tremendous impact on millions of Americans in our schools, workplaces, and communities, but we are just getting started. In 2023 alone, for example:

- Delta, in partnership with Operation HOPE and Fidelity Investments, established an Emergency Savings Program to help employees jumpstart their financial wellness journey in

January 2023. So far, more than 20% of its workforce—21,500 employees—have completed the financial skills, learning, and coaching steps to increase their financial knowledge and earn $1,000 from Delta to fund their rainy-day accounts. Moreover, participants have contributed an average of $1,061 of their own money to date—well above the required $250 contribution—and reported a 62% increase in their sense of financial control and a 139% increase in feeling able to save for other goals. Learn more about the program at deltafinancialwellness.com.

- Walmart and Khan Academy joined forces to offer a new, free financial literacy course for Walmart's associates, customers, and communities. The course offers articles, videos, and exercises to master personal financial capabilities, reduce stress, and make choices that lead to a healthier financial future. Launched in July 2023, the initiative has the potential to reach millions of people. Anyone can take the course for free at www.khanacademy.org/college-careers-more/financial-literacy.

- Dow Jones recently announced a new content offering dedicated to delivering financial literacy information, tools, and resources. Through this initiative, which will be launched in 2024, Dow Jones will leverage its portfolio of premium publications to provide access to essential information that will help empower and educate people about managing their finances.

- Operation HOPE, through its financial coaching and literacy programs, helps uplift thousands of people each year by teaching them how to improve their credit scores, increase their savings, and reduce their debt. In 2023, Operation HOPE delivered 278,369 financial coaching services to 56,793 individual clients. Clients improved their credit scores by an average of 41 points, with 25% of clients seeing an increase between 51 and 100 points; increased median savings by $1,116; and decreased their median debt by $1,892. More than 20% of clients now have three months of savings for an emergency, versus 11% before working with Operation HOPE coaches. In addition to FL4A, Operation HOPE has established initiatives such as the 1865 Project, which is determined to complete the mission of the Freedman's Bank established by President Lincoln; One Million Black Businesses (1MBB), which has been responsible for the creation of over 400,000 Black-owned businesses in the last two years alone; and HOPE Inside, a program that, at the end of 2023, has put 285 Operation HOPE branches inside banks, corporate headquarters, government offices, and similar venues to offer free financial coaching to company employees and customers. These are just a handful of the life-changing impacts that Operation HOPE makes in carrying out its mission.

Looking ahead, Financial Literacy for All will be expanding our focus and mobilizing our coalition to foster learning, collaboration, and inspiration among members. With our members' individual and collective firepower and reach, national amplification and awareness of our mission, and all that we have in store as we pursue our mission, we are confident that we can be a driving force in creating pivotal, lasting change by ensuring financial literacy for everyone in our nation.

For more information, including a resource library filled with free, helpful financial literacy materials, visit fl4a.org.

Acknowledgments

Frist and foremost, I would like to thank my amazing wife, Chaitra Bryant, for being a centered, high-frequency, stabilizing force and nourishing safe haven for me. You are the butterfly to my eagle. Your support and encouragement keep me focused and fueled. Your tips on healthy living and overall wellness help me keep an aggressive schedule and achieve a sense of balance and fulfillment. So much of my time is spent advocating for and taking care of others, but it is you who takes care of me. Thank you so much, love.

Special thanks to my family for their love and support, including my mother- and father-in-love, Dr. David Dalton and Mrs. Amy "Penny-Mom" Dalton; my brother, Dave Harris; sisters, Mara Hoskins and Arlene Hayes; my nephew, Mason Dalton; and, posthumously, my mother, Juanita Smith, and my father, Johnie Will Smith.

To my mentor, personal hero, and friend, civil rights icon, and HOPE's Global Spokesman Ambassador Andrew Young, who has helped to mentor, shape, and guide me in my adult life.

Special thanks to Bishop T.D. Jakes for sharing your wisdom and providing special spiritual inspiration for not only this book but also for my life's work. Thank you for being such a good friend. You are a selfless saint in this world.

To my late, great friend Tommy Dortch Jr., who was always down with the community, and, often, as a point of true inspiration, got caught in public "trying to do some good," to quote my friend Chelsea Clinton.

To those who have dedicated their lives to be part of my lifelong mission to eradicate poverty, those who fight with me in the trenches at Operation HOPE, Inc., I say, thank you: Brian Betts, Rod McGrew, Rachael Doff, Lance Triggs, Mary Ehrsam, Jena Roscoe, Sirjames Buchanon, Kevin Boucher, Jennifer Wolford, Nicole Pietro, Ed Eberhart, Keith Harris, Eric Kaplan, Tim Crockett, Debbie Fiddyment, Tina Fair, Debra Collins, Bill Fair, Louis Deas, and the entire, past, and present at Operation HOPE. You are my "special forces" unit and I am proud to work alongside each of you.

Special thanks to the members of Financial Literacy for All initiative, cofounded and chaired by myself and Walmart CEO Doug McMillon, who agree that financial literacy is the civil rights issue of our time, including American Express—Stephen Squeri, Ares—Michael Arougheti, Bank of America—Brian Moynihan, BlackRock—Larry Fink, Council for Economic Education—Nan Morrison, Delta—Ed Bastian, Denison Yachting—Bob Denison, Disney—Bob Iger, Dow Jones—Almar Latour, Edward Jones— Penny Pennington, FICO—Will Lansing, First Horizon—Bryan Jordan, General Motors—Mary Barra, Hershey—Michele Buck, iHeartRadio—Bob Pittman, JP Morgan Chase—Jamie Dimon, Khan Academy—Sal Khan, Mastercard—Michael Miebach, McDonald's—Chris Kempczinski, Moderna—Stephane Bancel, NASCAR—Steve Phelps, Nasdaq—Adena Friedman, Navy Federal Credit Union—Mary MacDuffie, NBA—Adam Silver,

Nextdoor—Sarah Friar, NFL—Roger Goodell, Nike—John Donahoe, Paramount—Bob Bakish, PayPal—Alex Chriss, Santander—Tim Wennes, Shopify—Tobi Lütke, Synchrony—Brian Doubles, TIME for Kids—Edward Felsenthal, Truist—Bill Rogers, Tyson—Donnie King, Uber—Dara Khosrowshahi, US Bank—Andrew Cecere, Verizon—Hans Vestberg, Visa—Ryan McInerney, Walgreens—Tim Wentworth, and Wells Fargo—Charlie Scharf.

To the Operation HOPE board members and partners (partial listing) who provide influence and resources, advancing the work, including Bryan Jordan, Michael Arougheti, Lisa Borders, Brad Smith, Frank Martell, Steve Ryan, Tim Welsh, Tim Wennes, Jed York, Ed Bastian, Craig Boundy, Janice Bryant-Howroyd, Chelsea Clinton, Bill Daley, Harley Finkelstein, Henry Ford, III, Roger Goodell, Linda Kirkpatrick, William Lansing, Aron Levine, Mike Maples, Curt Myers, former US Comptroller of the Currency Joseph Otting, Steve Phelps, Tony Ressler, David Riley, Bill Rogers Jr., Jeff Schmid, Brad Smith, Dallas Tanner, Carlos Vazquez, Regina Benjamin, William Cheeks, Carol Clarke, Ken Corbin, Sherrice Davis, Kimberly Dorsett, Calvin Dunning, Derek Ellington, Art Faulkner, Arlen Gelbard, Staci Glenn-Short, Smokey Glover, Allan Kamensky, Edward Kramer, Robert Marchman, Eli Marks, Lissa Miller, David Mooney, Gina Proia, Brett Shaffer, Charmaine Ward, Yusuf, Sam Altman, Bob Pittman, Gail McGovern, Dr. Lisa Herring, Mayor Andre Dickens, Curt Meyers, Smokey Glover, Linda Kirkpatrick, Shamina Singh, Michael Labriola, John Turner, Leroy Abrahams, Mercedes Garcia, Albert Bourla, Brian Chesky, HUD Secretary Marcia Fudge, Acting Comptroller Michael Hsu, US Treasury Deputy Secretary Wally Adeyemo, Chris Gorman, Tim Mapes, Joanne Smith, Darlene Goins, Carol Tomé, Dan Cathy, Steven Price, and countless others.

To the amazing supporters and friends of me and the Silver Rights Movement, including (but certainly not limited to) Michael Milken, Herb Allen III, Dr. Cecil "Chip" Murray, Roland Martin, Clifford "Tip—T.I." Harris, Charlamagne Tha God, Killer Mike, Ajay Banga, US Senator Raphael Warnock, US Senator Bill Cassidy, SBA administrator Isabel Guzman, Stephanie Ruhle, Atlanta Mayor Andre Dickens, Henry Kravis, Dr. George French, Strive Misiyiwa, Jay Clayton, Toby Shannon, Mellody Hobson, Reggie Jackson, Alex Rodriguez, Barry Wides, Anthony Scaramucci, Frank Holland, A. G. Salzberger, Mick Mulvaney, Cesar Conde, KC Sullivan, Mary Duffy, Dan Colarusso, Janean Lewis, Courtney English, and many others.

To my publishing and marketing/public relations teams who work tirelessly to package and promote the message I want to share with the world, including Brian Neill, Danielle Goodman, Lalohni Campbell, Bill Mendel, Sarah Trout, Heather Pink, and Christian Dear.

Heartfelt thanks to those who took the time to read early releases of the book, and who provided valuable feedback and statements of support, including Delta CEO Ed Bastian; Chase CEO Jamie Dimon; Nextdoor CEO Sarah Friar; Bishop T. D. Jakes; Truist chairman and CEO Bill Rogers Jr.; First Horizon Corporation chairman, president, and CEO Bryan Jordan; chairman and CEO iHeartMedia Bob Pittman; former CEO of PayPal Dan Schulman; U.S. Bancorp vice chair Tim Welsh; and media mogul, best-selling author, and TV/radio host Charlamagne Tha God; among others.

To my extended family at CNBC, led by KC Sullivan and Mary Duffy, along with some of the best on-air and behind the scenes talent in the business and the amazing crew at CNBC Squawkbox and Last Call, including Andrew Ross Sorkin, Rebecca Quick, Joe Kernan, Jacqueline Corba, Anne Tironi, Maxwell Meyers, Chelsea Whittemore, and Brian Sullivan. Thank you for welcoming me as a regular guest and for fostering a platform that embraces the sharing of diverse and disruptive perspectives.

To the leadership and team at The Promise Homes Company including Shawn Horwitz, Clayton Wyatt, Jake Keating, Erick Wilson, Randall Mason, Kyle Bryant, Scott Beck, Nylah Oliver, Cynthia Quick, Garrett Doff, Bernard Rayford, Blanca Carbajal, Michelle Childs, Zana Creary, Chasidy Moore, Lisa Gonzalez, Q Huntley, Mariah Kevinezz, Keiya Bailey, Chad DeWitt, and Demetrius Myatt, and CIM Group leadership including Richard Ressler, Shaul Kuba, Khalil Clements, Avi Shemesh, Robert Dupree, Steve Altebrando, Chris Allman. Thank you for your vision, investment, and dedication to creating a sustainable housing model focused on the advancement and financial uplift of its residents.

And finally, to all of my life teachers, mentors, and inspirers who have helped to educate me, formally and informally, to success . . . up from nothing, along the way: thank you for investing in me.

For anyone who has leaned in to advance the mission of HOPE, my life's work, but who are not mentioned here by name, please blame it on my head, not my heart. I remain eternally grateful to all who have been part of my journey.

About the Author

John Hope Bryant is an American entrepreneur, thought leader, philanthropic executive, and economic optimist.

Bryant is a CNBC Contributor, host of the iHeart Radio podcast, "Money and Wealth with John Hope Bryant," and a best-selling author of six books, including this one, *Financial Literacy For All*. He is one of the only Black bestselling authors on economics and business leadership in the world today.

Referred to as the "conscience of capitalism" by numerous Fortune 500 CEOs, Bryant is the founder, chairman, and chief executive officer of Operation HOPE, Inc. the nation's largest on-the-ground nonprofit provider of financial literacy. Operation HOPE is working to level the opportunity playing field for underserved America, connecting communities to the private sector through inclusive capitalism, at scale. In 2024 TIME Magazine elected him to the inaugural class of "The Closers"—a group of 18 extraordinary global leaders working to close the racial wealth gap.

Bryant is also chairman and chief executive officer of John Hope Bryant Holdings, Bryant Group Ventures, and executive chairman of The Promise Homes Company (Promise Homes), the largest for-profit minority-controlled owner of institutional-quality, single-family residential rental homes in the U.S. In December 2021, Bryant recapitalized Promise Homes into a new Promise Homes Co. joint venture, successfully closing a $200M credit facility to grow the new housing joint venture. According to Black Enterprise, it was one of the largest capital raises by a Black-owned company in more than a decade.

Organizations founded by Bryant have provided more than $4.2 billion in capital for the underserved over the past three decades. The 1 Million Black Businesses Initiative (1MBB), conceived by Bryant and Shopify founder and CEO Tobi Lütke, was launched in October 2020, and has since started, served, or scaled nearly 400,000 Black-owned businesses, representing 12% of all Black businesses in America. On May 2, 2023, 1MBB was recognized by Fast Company with the 2023 'World Changing Ideas' Award. Bryant also co-founded the Financial Literacy for All Initiative with Walmart CEO Doug McMillion, a movement of Fortune 500 executives united in leveraging their brands to embed financial literacy into U.S. culture.

Bryant's financial empowerment work has been recognized by five U.S. presidents. He has served as an advisor to three sitting U.S. presidents representing both parties. In 2021, Bryant was called upon by U.S. Treasury officials to help design the Payroll Protection Program (PPP), which helped millions of small businesses and entrepreneurs survive during the COVID-19 pandemic.

In 2016, Bryant influenced U.S. Treasury Secretary Jack Lew to rename the Treasury Annex Building to the Freedman's Bank Building, in honor of the Freedman's Bank created by President Lincoln, designed to teach newly freed slaves about money. He is the only U.S. citizen to inspire the renaming of a building on the White House campus. Bryant also inspired the Treasury Department to host a Freedman's Bank Forum, which has continued annually under successive administrations.

In 2008, Bryant inspired President George W. Bush to make financial literacy the official policy of the U.S. federal government. Following 9/11, Bryant also worked with the Bush Administration to create a new federal policy framework for financial disaster preparedness, response, and recovery, resulting in a first-ever partnership with the U.S. Department of Homeland Security/ FEMA and Operation HOPE.

Bryant has received hundreds of awards and citations for his work, including Oprah Winfrey's "Use Your Life" Award, and the "John Sherman Award for Excellence in Financial Education" from the U.S. Department of Treasury. He was part of TIME Magazine's inaugural class of "50 Leaders for the Future" in 1994, alongside Bill Gates, Jamie Dimon, John F. Kennedy, Jr., Maya Lin, and Wynton Marsalis, and American Banker named him "Innovator of the Year" in 2016.

In 2019, the City of Atlanta, where Operation HOPE is based, designated April 15 as "John Hope Bryant Day." Operation HOPE and Bryant are also a permanent part of the Smithsonian African American Museum in Washington D.C.

In April 2017, Bryant, with support from his friend, HOPE board member and First Horizon Bank CEO Bryan Jordan, inspired a historical marker to recognize the final flight of Dr. Martin Luther King, Jr., to Memphis on April 3, 1968. The marker was installed at the Memphis International Airport 49 years to the day that Eastern Flight 381 arrived from Atlanta.

Bryant is a LinkedIn Influencer, and was selected as one of LinkedIn's "Top 10 Voices." His social media video series, "Straight Talk with John Hope Bryant," has received over 100 million views, which led to a Facebook-sponsored episodic streaming series entitled, 'Delivering The Memo,' inspired by Bryant's bestselling book, *The Memo*. He has over three million followers across his social media platforms.

John Hope Bryant was born on February 6, 1966, in Los Angeles, CA. He and his wife Chaitra Dalton Bryant reside in Atlanta.

Bibliography

Financial Literacy For All: Disrupting Struggle, Advancing Financial Freedom, and Building a New American Middle Class (Wiley, 2024)

Up from Nothing: The Untold Story of How We (All) Succeed (Berrett-Koehler, 2020)

The Memo: Five Rules for Your Economic Liberation (Berrett-Koehler, 2017)

How the Poor Can Save Capitalism: Rebuilding the Path to the Middle Class (Berrett-Koehler, 2014)

LOVE LEADERSHIP: The New Way to Lead in a Fear-Based World (Jossey-Bass, 2009)

Index